Village Life
in
SOUTH
INDIA

Village Life
in
SOUTH
INDIA

Cultural Design and Environmental Variation

ALAN R. BEALS

ALDINETRANSACTION
A Division of Transaction Publishers
New Brunswick (U.S.A.) and London (U.K.)

Library of Congress Catalog Number: 2011030250
ISBN 978-1-4128-4273-0
Printed in the United States of America

Library of Congress Cataloging-in-Publication Data

Beals, Alan R.
    Village life in south India : cultural design and environmental varia-
    tion / Alan R. Beals.
        p. cm.
    Includes index.
    ISBN 978-1-4128-4273-0
    1. Villages--India, South. I. Title.

HN683.B43 2011
307.76'209548--dc23

                                                        2011030250

Contents

Foreword

Of the world's major civilizations, the Indian is perhaps the most difficult for Westerners to comprehend. The formal structure of castes with their apparent fixity, the strong sense of hierarchy supported ritually by the concept of pollution, the religious belief in reincarnation as both a justification for one's present condition and as a motivation for proper conduct, are all alien to our way of thinking. The peculiarities of Indian culture have been known to the West since Megasthenes, the Greek emissary, wrote on India about 300 years B.C. Early Western descriptions, generalized and remote from daily realities, have exaggerated these differences rather than promoted understanding. Indian scholars, steeped in their own traditions and viewpoints, offering descriptions of the system as a theoretical and theological construct, have hardly been more helpful.

To understand how the Indian culture actually operates in the daily life of the ordinary person, it was necessary to have the detailed analyses of social anthropologists. Over the past four decades, many studies of Indian villages have shown us how life is actually conducted within their culturally defined universe. Yet its forms have still remained enigmatic, a seemingly inefficient way of organizing peasant society.

Alan Beals, by bringing an ecological approach to the examination of Indian rural life, shows us the functional effectiveness of these traditional institutions and demonstrates their adaptive flexibility. Beals portrays three communities he has studied intensively, to indicate both the consistencies and the variations in South Indian village life. He shows how caste interrelationships create a stable set of mutual obligations, how these are maintained by concepts of proper religiously sanctioned behavior, how the *jati* or sub-castes establish community bonds, and above all, how these various relationships and involvements alter under differing environmental circumstances.

There are two basic parameters to this environmental variation: the characteristics of the land from which sustenance is derived through the application of human effort, and the variant effects of urban centers, whether exercised through political power, economic involvement, or religious influence. Intra-village caste relationships, to take one important example, are shaped by these forces. They are patterned by such remote concepts—remote from the standpoint of caste theory—as the kinds of soil and the slope of the land. Thus, matters like farm production, animal husbandry, caste organization and the institutions of authority are seen to adjust to the conformation of the local terrain; the very shape of the Indian village, both literally as it can be mapped on the ground and figuratively as it is viewed in Indian thought, conforms to environmental pressures.

Beals not only demonstrates the functional effectiveness of social institutions, but gives us an appreciation of the Indian world view. As he says, the Indian viewpoint is more systems-oriented and ecological in its formulation than is the characteristic understanding of Western man. The Hindu sense of unity with nature provides a recognition of the integration of life that is only now taking prominence in our scientific thought with the advent of an ecological theory.

Worlds of Man is a series designed to further this ecological understanding, cast in a scientific rather than a theological mode. In so doing, we are perhaps bringing old verities into a modern frame of reference, for this is not the first of the native peoples described in this series who have shared an essentially ecological understanding of their world. The fact that such ecological perceptions are part of folk wisdom does not make it less important that they become central to anthropological understanding as well.

WALTER GOLDSCHMIDT

Introduction

In his ancient treatise on the law, Baudhayana identified five characteristics which differentiated South Indian civilization from the societies that surrounded it: dining with persons not initiated into the diner's caste or religious sect, dining with women, eating food kept overnight, marrying the daughter of a maternal uncle, and marrying the daughter of a paternal aunt. Although not all modern scholars regard South India as sufficiently different or sufficiently uniform to justify treating it independently of the rest of Indian civilization, most would acknowledge the existence of distinctive characteristics of the kind listed by Baudhayana. Often, South India is defined as a place where Dravidian languages, different from the Indo-Europen languages of northern India, are spoken.

South India's civilization is old. King Solomon received shipments of peacocks and sandalwood from South India, and rice, peacocks, and sandalwod shipped to Babylon before the fifth century B.C. bore Dravidian names. There is evidence of trade between China and South India as early as 700 B.C. Roman coins unearthed in South India testify to the existence of direct or indirect trade with the Roman Empire. For two or three thousand years, cities have been built, art forms have developed, religions have grown and spread, and empires have flourished and collapsed in South India.

Throughout this time the foundation of South Indian civilization has been the rural village community—a cluster of mud, stone, and thatched buildings housing from 50 to 2,000 people and their cattle. Despite constant change, famine, war, epidemic, and flood, the rural community has maintained its cup of life unbroken through the centuries. The ancient gods, altered but still identifiable, still rule the village temple; the same bullocks pull the farmer's plow; the same houses line the village streets; and the same aggressive, lively people described in ancient poems fill the village with their word and song, even though the song is now from the latest motion picture.

The South Indian village is one of the great, enduring works of humanity. Its passage through the shoals of time testifies to the success of South Indian civilization in managing the problems of survival. South Indians may at times have failed to cope with the stresses of their ever-changing environment. Vital resources may have been exhausted or destroyed. Thus far, however, the people have been able to remedy such mistakes and to maintain unbroken the relationships to the world around them that preserve the essence of their civilization as well as the environmental assets on which the continuation of their way of life depends.

To a person like me who has spent four years immersed in the cowdung and poetry of South Indian villages, the question of how they endure and persist seems neither trivial nor irrelevant. Perhaps the fate of the newer civilizations of Europe and America and of the human species itself depends on our ability to shape our civilization as cleverly and effectively as the South Indians shaped theirs three thousand years ago. The purpose of this book is to examine the kinds of relationships that exist between South Indian villages and the world around them in order to understand their successful persistence in an uncertain world.

Because civilization in South India involves thousands of villages, towns, and cities occupied by millions of people and because much of the basic research concerning the history and nature of this society remains to be done, this small volume cannot contain anything like a complete or final statement. It can only represent a beginning, a few tentative observations on the nature of South Indian villages and their external relationships. Because my own knowledge and experience is based primarily on the study of three villages in different parts of Mysore State, much of what is written here is based on an understanding of the ecological systems of which those villages form a part. Although I have tried to consider the general significance for South India of the patterns of life encountered in the three villages, many of my conclusions must be considered hypothetical and tentative. South India is a place of extraordinary cultural and environmental diversity, and almost every village contains exceptions to items that might appear on any list of "typical" characteristics. Some complexities of the habitat are explored in the following section.

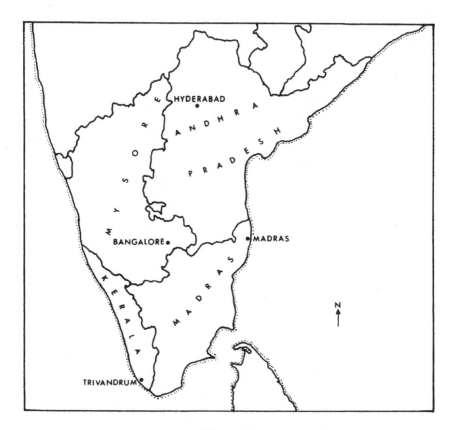

Figure 1

South India is made up of the cultural and linguistic provinces of Madras, Kerala, Mysore and Andhra. (See Figure 1) These provinces now form linguistic states based on the four major Dravidian languages: Tamil in Madras; Malayalam in Kerala; Kannada in Mysore; and Telugu in Andhra. But South India does not exist independently of the rest of India or the rest of the world. Dravidian civilization has contributed much to the civilization of

India, and in turn it has developed its basic features while closely associated with other regions and other cultures. If we set South India apart from the rest of India and from the other civilizations of man, we do so largely as a matter of convenience.

Throughout history, polyglot empires have spread across South India, endured for centuries, and vanished, leaving behind petty states and chiefdoms. Religious movements have engendered wars, culminating in formal and informal agreements to practice mutual toleration.

Despite war and conflict, each year thousands of pilgrims have traveled hundreds of miles to worship at religious shrines. Young brides, carefully veiled and shielded from supernatural harm, have moved twenty, thirty, even one hundred miles from their birthplaces to the family homes of their husbands. Tradesmen carrying cloth, spices, jewelry, and other portable and imperishable goods have traveled safely across the country, visiting markets and villages. Entertainers, religious mendicants, beggars, snake catchers, duck herders, and flute makers have moved routinely on their rounds. Linguistic, religious, and political distinctions divide South India, but pilgrimage, marriage, and trade reunite the fragments.

South India is perhaps best understood when compared with the more familiar southern Europe. Traditionally, southern Europe was united by the Roman Catholic church and its peoples communicated by means of Latin. South India was united by the spread of Brahmans and other religious practitioners, who represented a variety of sects but communicated a common religious and philosophical heritage in Sanskrit. Such states as the Holy Roman Empire periodically united parts of southern Europe; such states as the Vijayanagar Empire united parts of South India. In southern Europe, parochialism, a tendency to live and marry within a single parish, augmented the value of the church as a means of holding things together. In South India, cosmopolitanism, stemming from the presence of many different castes and occupations and the practice of marrying outside the village, made a strong religious organization and a strong state less essential to the preservation of cultural unity.

Southern Europe and South India were both located on the trade routes between China and northern Europe. Ships from Malaya brought cargo to South Indian ports, from which it was carried overland to the west coast and picked up by Arab vessels which carried it to East Africa and the Red Sea. From there, it moved across the Mediterranean to southern European ports and across southern Europe to the North Atlantic. South India and southern Europe were on the periphery of great Muslim empires. Despite recurrent religious wars, in South India, unlike southern Europe, Muslims came to be valued for their distinctive contributions to society.

A perhaps critical difference between South India and other regions of the world where complex civilizations have developed is its geographical diversity and the comparative isolation of mountain-enclosed subregions in every part of the area. The capitals of Mediterranean civilization had easy access to each other via the Mediterranean Sea. North Indian civilization was centered on the flat and geographically homogeneous Indo-Gangetic Plain. The great river valleys of China also permitted easy access and communication across great regions. It may be that only in ancient Middle America, Peru, and West Africa did major civilizations develop in the midst of such geographical diversity as characterizes South India.

GEOGRAPHY AND SETTLEMENT

South India is guarded from the north by transverse mountain ranges running from east to west across the Indian triangle. The central part of South India is a plateau sloping toward the east and cut off from the coastal regions by eastern and western mountain ranges. While parts of the east coast are mountainous, most of the coastal regions of Madras and Andhra are flat, well-watered plains suitable for rice agriculture. (See Figure 2) In such "rice bowls" as Tanjore, kingdoms have arisen and spread westward into the mountain and plateau regions in efforts to gain control of the watersheds on which their livelihood was based. Over and over again, rugged terrain and the expense of maintaining control over the relatively worthless interior lands have caused withdrawal.

The more rugged and mountainous areas of South India are occupied by tribal peoples who have maintained their identity and way of life as small bands of hunters and gatherers. The mountain valleys and plateaus are occupied by relatively independent agri-

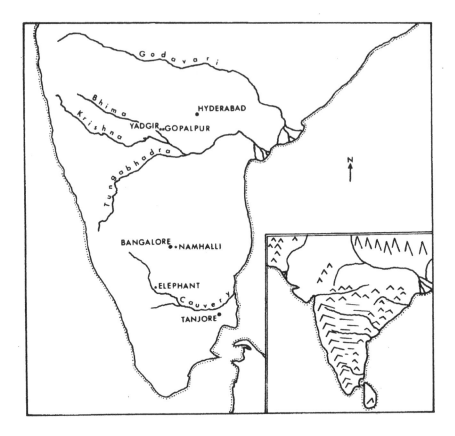

Figure 2

cultural communities and small states and chiefdoms. Such "tribal" peoples engage in trade with the peoples of the plains and have borrowed many of their ideas and practices from them. Although recent improvements in weaponry and communication have brought the "advantages" of centralized government to the tribal peoples, their unique ways of life still persist in many regions.

The eastern mountains are arid, rocky, and thinly populated. Beyond the mountains are the relatively dry plateau regions of Andhra and Mysore. Here, large and small irrigation works permit the development of complex forms of rice and garden agriculture. The population is denser than that of the mountains, and there are sizable cities. Mountain ranges and river gorges slice the plateau regions into small sections and render communication difficult.

The history of Mysore and Andhra has been one of small feuding states, each centered upon a town or small city. As in ancient Peru, there were periodic unifications, but these often meant nothing more than the exacting of tribute from subordinate chiefs and princelings, who were themselves engaged in extracting tribute from their own poorly controlled villages and towns.

The mountains and "rainy lands" of western Mysore form a barrier between east and west. Here again, tribal peoples flourish and there are dozens of unique and virtually unstudied groups. The western slopes of the mountains plunge directly into the sea, forming a series of steep valleys that run to the ocean. Formerly, almost every valley harbored a separate kingdom that fought wars and exacted tribute from its neighbors. Rugged as they are, the coastal lands (Malabar and Kerala) are highly productive. From the earliest times, Malabar was an important source of pepper, cardamon, and other spices.

Across South India, variations in rainfall, geographical barriers, and other physiographic features have created a variety of ecological niches and zones, some of which are difficult of access. The need to adapt to local conditions has compelled each village and region to develop its own unique adjustments. Still, there are many characteristics that unite large sections of South India: a particular style of plow agriculture, a particular set of religious concepts and interpretations, a tendency to prefer marriage with a sister's daughter, mother's brother's daughter, or father's sister's daughter, and the division of people into endogamous (inmarrying) castes. Some of South India's characteristics exist in other parts of India and of the world. Still, in South India these characteristics go together in a different way.

In view of the complexity of the South Indian environment and the diversity of its cultures, it is difficult to generalize about the region as a whole. By describing particular villages and the ways in which they have come to terms with the world, a sense of unified ecological systems can be preserved. While no village is "normal" or "typical" in a statistical sense, each is likely to be representative of a large class of relatively similar villages. The strategy of this book, then, is to focus upon three villages and, where relevant, to discuss the extent to which the things that happen in them are representative of things that happen elsewhere as well.

The three villages are Elephant, Namhalli, and Gopalpur (see

Map, p. 14). They are located in different parts of Mysore State, and their inhabitants angrily deny that there are any important resemblances among them. The citizens of Namhalli view the people of Elephant and Gopalpur as "jungly" (barbaric and uncivilized). The citizens of Elephant regard outsiders as sinful and irreligious. In Gopalpur, an intense loyalty to the ancient kingdom of which the village was once a part demands that all outsiders be considered foreigners.

Versions of Kannada, the official language of Mysore State, are spoken in all three villages. They share similar crops and similar agricultural techniques. They are part of the same bureaucratic and governmental structure, although Elephant is technically located in Madras rather than Mysore. Caste, or more correctly, *jati* (pronounced "jahti"), is a feature of all three communities, although, as is the case for many other South Indian villages and hamlets, Elephant's regular residents are members of only one jati. Ways of building houses, ways of dressing, postures, ways of making and using tools, domesticated animals, and many other features of daily life are similar among the three villages. Finally, despite powerful differences of opinion, the religious concepts and rituals followed in all three villages have a common philosophy and origin.

ELEPHANT

The correct name of Elephant is untranslatable. I have called it Elephant partly because it is regularly visited by herds of wild elephants and partly because a deaf old lady on a bus once scornfully translated its proper name as "one-and-a-half elephants." The village lies some 60 miles south of the city of Bangalore. It is situated just across the Madras-Mysore border, at the head of a small valley reaching downward into the gorge of the Cauvery River and surrounded by mountains and forests stretching to a distant blue horizon. In the forests are tigers and elephants. Tigers attack village cattle, and elephants may consume whole haystacks in a single raid.

In 1952, Elephant contained 66 households and 291 persons (4.41 persons per household). It had a high infant mortality and little access to any kind of modern medical care. Under such circumstances, a high birthrate is needed to maintain a stable population. Thus, over half the population consisted of young children, many destined never to reach maturity. Since 1941, Elephant had grown slightly as a result of immigration, but for the most part it had not been affected by the sharp increases of population characteristic of modernizing villages such as Namhalli. Lacking any school beyond a traditional religious "folk school" and having few economic, social, or political ties to any urban institutions, Elephant can be taken to represent a kind of village that was much more common one hundred or even five hundred years ago.

Elephant became accessible to modern influences in 1951, when a bus service was inaugurated between the nearby town of Tamarind and Bangalore. Previously, people from Elephant had purchased pottery, cloth, and a few other goods in Tamarind, and few found any need to go farther. From Tamarind, stone staircases lead up the almost vertical face of a mountainside to the hill-top where Elephant lies hidden under flowering and fruiting trees. Its streets are laid out casually on the rough terrain.

In 1952, the houses that lined the streets were one-room buildings made of earth moistened and pressed into the shape of walls. Floors were of gravel, covered with a paste of cowdung, and roofs were of handmade "country" tile. Women in Elephant wore coarsely woven cotton saris, and many of the men wore sleeveless shirts and strips of cloth passed between their legs rather than the more expensive long-sleeved shirts and short trousers. Those who had something to do with the outside world sometimes affected more elegant clothing, but in general the people seemed to be more poorly dressed than in most parts of South India.

There was one large and expensive building in the village. This was the *mathe*, a structure designed to feed and house pilgrims. The mathe represented a dream of the people of Elephant, a dream of former times when wealthy pilgrims traveled the road from Tamarind to visit holy places in the woods. Elephant's people planned to construct a new and better mathe that would again attract a flow of pilgrims. The offerings and contributions of the pilgrims, to say nothing of the resulting business opportunities, would bring prosperity to the village.

Dressed in the bright orange regalia of the Hindu Lingayat sect, the Svamiji served as parish priest in Elephant and several surrounding villages. As *guru*, it was his task to teach the proper way of life to his people and to serve as priest at birth, marriage, and funeral ceremonies. Since the Svamiji was a *viractasvami*, a man who could never marry, he occupied a higher position among Lingayat priests than would a married priest. To fulfill himself in his role, he required a larger and grander throne. The new mathe was to be such a throne.

Outside the village, terraced agricultural lands cling to the hillsides. Most of these lands are shaded by surviving forest trees or long-established tamarinds and mangoes. In 1952, several shallow wells were scattered through the village. Except for the Svamiji's well, all of these dried up during the hot season, and it became necessary for all except the Svamiji and a favored few to fetch water from the stream at Tamarind. Without water for bathing or drinking, let alone irrigation, Elephant was and is totally dependent on crops raised on the rocky hillsides during the rainy season.

Years ago, presumably before the British conquered Mysore in 1800, Elephant and some twenty other villages, forming a "country," were ruled by a chieftain named Thabbalamanda. According to local stories, Thabbalamanda raided Tamarind and other more distant centers until the Maharaja of Mysore sent in an army and killed him. Not long after this loss of independence, the British East India Company invaded Mysore and annexed Elephant and its country to Madras. Although these invasions had some impact on the manner in which Elephant's people paid taxes and, when the country was declared a reserved forest (comparable to a United States national forest), on its lands and resources, the great civilizing influence claimed by the rulers of Mysore and their British successors had little effect on Elephant or its country.

Villages remained remote and inaccessible even to each other. The various Svamijis dispensed the law and the truth as they always had. The crops grown and the techniques used in growing them remained unchanged. People in Elephant continued to pride themselves on their religiosity and to fortify their spiritual purity by confining almost all of their marirages and social contacts to a circle of five or six villages. While it is tempting to think of Elephant as a surviving representative of a time when India was underpopulated and every village was surrounded by forest, the truth is that Elephant and its country were never in the mainstream of South Indian culture. Here no imperial armies marched. Despite footprints and other signs supposedly left by the heroes of the *Mahabharata* and the *Ramayana*, India's great epic poems, bosky chieftains like Thabbalamanda probably represent the region's pinnacle of greatness.

GOPALPUR

Almost exactly halfway between Madras and Bombay, not far from the once famous cities of Badami, Bijapur, Golconda, Gulbarga, and Hampi, the Gopalpur region has lain in the mainstream of South Indian culture for millennia. People in Gopalpur have long been influenced by the great Muslim kingdoms of northern Mysore and Hyderabad. Their dialect of Kannada borrows heavily from the Hindi and Urdu spoken by the Muslim rulers, and they are contemptuous of those who speak only one or two languages. Educated people in the Gopalpur region speak Hindi or Urdu; even Brahmans fasten with delight on Persian poetry. Many speak Marathi or Tamil; all speak the Kannada and Telugu mother tongues.

In the Elephant region, the works of man still lie sheltered within the forest; in the Gopalpur region, the woodman's ax and the farmer's plow transformed the environment long ago. Forests and hillsides offer a barren tribute to a constant search for fuel; soils have been worn out, left to recover, and then worn out again. On every hillslope, decaying temples reflect the passage of Buddhists, Jains, Lingayats, and members of other now-forgotten sects. Outcrops of granite topped by palaces and defended by the rusting cannon of some former war testify to man's struggles for possession of this barren, central land. Here are the same walls, the same great domes, the same stone houses, and the same crooked streets that are found in Athens, Rome, and Alexandria. Broken temples, ruined palaces, and ancient mortuaries conceal long-abandoned art treasures, thus far protected from the ravages of tourism and theft.

In Gopalpur, a few poverty-stricken families live in thatched houses with mud walls, but most families live in stone fortresses, dark as dungeons and stained with the smoke of cooking fires. Light enters through five-inch holes high in the outer wall or through circular openings in the roof. The walls are made of stone, sometimes rough and sometimes dressed with hard steel tools introduced by the British. The flat roofs are built up of branches covered with a six-inch layer of clay. A single door, sometimes intricately carved, admits cattle and people to the dark interior. Cattle stalls, located at ground level occupy the center of the house and are surrounded by small rooms where women cook, grind flour, and lull their children to sleep in cradles hanging from the scabrous ceiling.

Clothing in Gopalpur follows traditional south Indian patterns. Women wear jewels in their ears and nose, silver belts and anklets, and glass bracelets. Men wear jewelry in their ears and silver arm-bands and waistcords. Women's *saris* are made of coarse cotton wrapped twice around and often drawn through the legs Mahratti style. Men wear heavy cotton *dhotis*, elaborately pleated and folded between their legs. Most men also wear a long turban, a woolen blanket or a gunnysack, and a pair of thick sandals. Such clothing suggests a degree of prosperity not evident in Elephant.

In 1960, Gopalpur had some 106 households containing 483 people (4.56 persons per household). Where almost all of the people in Elephant belong to the Lingayat jati, there are a variety of jatis in Gopalpur. Saltmakers farm and make salt; Farmers till the soil; Shepherds farm and raise sheep; Stoneworkers farm and build stone houses; and there are a variety of families of Brahmans, Lingayat Priests, Barbers, Washermen, Carpenters, Blacksmiths, Basket Weavers, and Leatherworkers, most of whom farm as well as carry out traditional tasks. Where leadership in Elephant is religious and vested primarily in the Svamiji, leadership in Gopalpur is secular, and in 1960 it was vested primarily in the person of the Brahman landlord who owned nearly one-sixth of the village lands.

Gopalpur contains an irrigation tank and some 100 acres of rice land. To the east, the soil is black and heavy. To the west, it is sandy and produces crops only during the rainy season. Here and there, wells are used to irrigate vegetable crops or raise seedlings for transplantation. For nine months out of the year, there is work in Gopalpur. But during the hot months—March, April, and May—the village becomes a desert. The days are cloudless, and the thermometer rapidly rises above 100°F. and remains there night and day. The government doctor in the nearby town of Yadgiri frequently records temperatures of 118°.

With continuing high mortality due to malaria, smallpox, and cholera, the Gopalpur region has not experienced rapid increases in population. In 1966, under the influence of modern medicine, infant mortality was beginning to fall, but the population was decreasing as a result of migration to Bombay. Apart from emigration, Gopalpur and its region have remained relatively untouched by the modern world. Wealthy landlords block the construction of schools and discourage government attempts at community development. The once great cities surrounding Gopalpur have shrunk or disappeared, and the only nearby metropolis is the city of Hyderabad, 100 miles to the east. Wide acres of sandy soil and the deep-cut ravines through which the rivers pass suggest that the agricultural wealth which once fueled some of the greatest empires known to man has dwindled. There remains, however, a consciousness of greatness and an arrogant disregard of the barbarians outside the gate.

NAMHALLI

A century ago, Bangalore was a small town and Namhalli a lonely village fortified with a fence of thorns. The comparatively cool climate of Bangalore and its accessibility to the sources of British strength in Madras caused it to attract a large British garrison. The active military were followed by retired colonels, missionaries, Tamil-speaking immigrants, schools, and ultimately factories.

People from Namhalli and other villages near Bangalore soon found themselves in a position to take advantage of schools and factories and to market their produce, particularly vegetables and fruits, in the city. Although Bangalore came to provide a source of traditional urban Indian knowledge and outlooks, it was also, from the beginning, a source of modern European and international viewpoints. By 1900, people from Namhalli were beginning to move into a modern and international channel. When World War II filled Bangalore with naively generous British and American soldiers who had been sent there for training and recuperation, Namhalli was able to display a hospitable and tolerant attitude toward the ways of foreigners. Where the Gopalpur region maintains the arrogance of ancient glory, Namhalli has won through to the economic and ideological blessings of that new international culture perhaps best represented by *Screen* magazine.

Men working in the fields are likely to wear short trousers and undershirts. When they go to the city, they wrap neatly pressed dhotis of fine cloth around their waists and put on long-sleeved shirts. A towel is carried over one shoulder to be draped over the head like a shawl if the heat becomes oppressive. A younger man going to the city wears long trousers cut to the latest international style, shoes with socks, and a shirt tucked into his trousers. So dressed, the citizens of Namhalli are indistinguishable from urban residents. Women wear short saris with petticoats and blouses with buttons. When dressed for a wedding or a trip to town, women from the village are as indistinguishable from their favorite Bombay film stars as it is possible to be.

Even the houses in Namhalli look urban. They are built in rows along streets that run at right angles to each other and are lined somewhat irregularly with trees. Adobe brick, plaster, whitewash, and machine-made tiles give many houses the look of urban bungalows. By 1966, chimneys, barred and shuttered windows, living room furniture, radios, electric lights, cement floors, electric fans, bicycles, and other urban appurtenances had given most houses a citified look. Traditional houses in Namhalli are built around three or four sides of a walled courtyard where cattle are kept.

In 1952, Namhalli contained 106 households and 603 people (5.53 persons per household), just about double its population in 1900. In 1960, Namhalli contained 113 households and 542 people (4.79 persons per household). The dwindling population is explained partly by emigration, with many families moving into housing colonies near the factories where they work, and partly by the use of various means of population control, ranging from infanticide to contraceptives. With excellent medical facilities available and a strong desire to purchase urban gimcracks and attend motion pictures, most of the younger people in Namhalli arrange to have small families.

Like Gopalpur, Namhalli comprises people from a variety of jatis, but there are more vegetarians in Namhalli because one of the large farmer jatis belongs, like the people of Elephant, to the vegetarian Lingayat sect.

ECOLOGY

Individual agricultural villages, such as Elephant, Namhalli, and Gopalpur, can be regarded as representing South Indian civilization in the sense that they are the result of that civilization's impact on particular places. If we regard South Indian civilization as a design for human activity, then each hamlet, village, town, or city within it represents the basic plan as it has been modified to take particular local circumstances into account. Agricultural villages can be regarded as a basic feature of South Indian civilization because cities, towns and all the other complex institutional features of that civilization are ultimately dependent on the villages for the food energy that maintains them. Principally through the production of grain crops, the village captures energy from the sun, and this energy, in the form of agricultural produce, provides the fuel that maintains armies, kings, temples, and all the other complicated institutions of civilization.

Fundamental to an explanation of the long-term persistence of South Indian civilization is an explanation of the pattern of life in the agricultural villages that contribute the energy for its maintenance. Understanding the agricultural villages depends, in turn, on understanding the complicated sets of relationships that permit their development and perpetuation. The persistence of a particular village in a particular spot is evidence that the successive groups of people living there have established sufficiently consistent relationships among themselves and with the world around them to permit their survival.

The emphasis of this book is upon the relationships between villages and their various environments. Here the basic concept is that of "ecology." In the biological sciences, "ecology" is defined as the study of the web of relationships that unite into "community," or ecosystem, particular environments and the plant and animal species that occupy them. In this approach, the characteristics of any particular plant or animal species are understood as the result of complex interactions with the environment and among the different species. "Village ecology" is the study of the complex system of relationships that is formed when a village is established in a particular environment.

Because each village and its environment form a single, complicated, constantly changing organization, the anthropologist who seeks to understand the ecosystem of which the community is a component finds himself in the same position as an eight-year-old trying to understand an alarm clock by taking it apart. The functioning of the clock depends on its unity, on the relationship of its parts. When this fragile unity is disrupted nothing remains but an inexplicable jumble of lifeless nuts and gears. If we are to understand an alarm clock or an ecosystem, we must dissect it carefully, remembering the relationships among its parts and, in the end, reassembling it so it works as well as ever. However, because an ecosystem is an organic rather than a mechanical system, its parts are fluid and flexible, overlapping each other, merging into each other, and connecting with each other in extraordinary and complicated ways.

How, then, does one begin to describe the web of relationships constituting the ecosystem of a village? For present purposes, I have conceived of a village as a product of the interaction of a cultural tradition, a set of people, and an environment. In historical or developmental terms, a village comes into being when a particular group of people establish themselves in a particular place and begin to carry out activities which they have learned as part of the cultural tradition of some other settlement. The tradition contains certain basic ideas about the nature of villages and the purposes of human endeavor, as well as a set of technologies, or ways of coping with the environment. As people begin to apply these technologies, they establish relationships between themselves and the environment. Some of the technologies learned elsewhere prove ineffective and new ones have to be borrowed or invented. The application of these technologies produces changes in the environment, and these changes also affect the developing technology of the village. Ultimately, if all goes well, the relationships between the village and its environment become sufficiently stable to endure and the village takes its place as a permanent part of the ecosystem.

In line with this reasoning, Chapter 1 presents a summary of the basic ideas that South Indian villagers use in coming to terms with the world around them. Chapter 2 deals more specifically with the ways in which the basic structure or plan that the South Indian village derives from the cultural traditions of South Indian civilization finds particular expression in Elephant, Namhalli, and Gopalpur. At this point the stage is set, but the problems of describing the relationships of the villages to their environments remain. Is there any reasonable way of dividing the environment into parts that may be discussed independently of one another?

At the outset, the perpetuation of the village can be viewed as dependent upon the capacity of its people to meet two fundamental requirements: they must be successful in establishing productive relationships with the surrounding lands and they must obtain the human material required to perform the tasks on which the survival of the village depends. Chapter 3, then, deals with the various technologies, mostly agricultural, that are available within the cultural traditions of South Indian civilization. Chapter 4 considers the application of these technologies to the various lands, resources, and plant and animal species that are found within the boundaries of each village. It also considers the impact of technology on the village and its ecological relationships. In effect, Chapter 4 describes the critical intersection between the ideas that people have about the things that should be done and the particular natural environment within which those ideas are applied.

Chapter 5 deals with the special problems involved in producing, training, and maintaining the human membership required for the perpetuation of the village. Here the concept of "human environment" is used, perhaps in a peculiar sense, to refer to those biological characteristics and limitations of the human species that must be dealt with if the village is to maintain its membership. Chapters 6 and 7 consider the special technologies that are used to establish and maintain the relationships among villages in a region which permit the exchange of personnel and a wide variety of goods and services. Beyond the world of villages and of relationships among them lies the more complicated world of regional, national, and even worldwide civilization. Chapters 8 and 9 deal with the relationships between the village and the towns, cities, and governmental and religious institutions that directly affect it.

In recent years the South Indian village, together with all the other villages and settled places of the world, has come under the influence of those snowballing changes in culture and technology that are called "modernization" and "urbanization." Chapter 10 deals with the new kinds of ecological relationships that take form as the village becomes a participant in the modern world and in new kinds of urban environments.

Although each village uses different technologies and establishes different kinds of ecological relationships with the different aspects of its environment described in Chapters 2 through 10, the establishment of relationships with any one aspect of the environment has implications for the kind of relationships that can be established with any other. Chapter 11 is an attempt to reassemble the clock, to consider the overall pattern of the village and its environment conceived as a single complex system.

Chapter 1

THE SOUTH INDIAN WORLD

Human beings harbor dreams and make maps, and few doubt that the dreams and maps are more real than the confused territory they represent. Men who establish villages bring with them ideas about the world and what should be accomplished within it. From the interaction of these ideas with the cutting edge of reality, every village develops a patern of relationships with the environment and within itself that permits it to survive, to maintain what Ralph Linton called "the things that make life worth living," and to remain representative of its civilization.

A poet living in Elephant describes his world as follows:

> Above the stream bank's joining
> Is the place called Tamarind.
> Sixteen shops are in its streets.
> Big business is going on.
>
> Heaped with fruits and vegetables,
> Buses daily reach the town.
> A coconut worth an anna
> Sells for six or more.
>
> Villagers, loud and quarrelsome,
> Walking with loads on their heads,
> Take leave of the town,
> Come to the stream that flows like a river.

Fording the stream,
They come to Kasettypur hamlet.
On the hilltop, far above,
Elephant can be seen.

Climb and climb
The long stone stairways.
Near the top is the boundary,
Elephant just beyond.

Fifty-five families in the village,
Farmers all of them.
Singing plowing songs, they grow millet.
Fearless, they live in pride.

The tall landlord, the short village messenger,
The deaf chieftain. These three
Have joined the five council members
And increased village taxes.

If the children's happy family life is ruined,
These elders hear the cries and come running.
For a dirty sixty rupees,
They wreck the family completely.

When elephants and wild boars cause commotion,
The elders run amok protecting their fields.
Called to worship God in the temple,
They sleep by the side of their wives.

Stand in the village, look to the right.
Toward the hilltop is Attinatha village.
To the left
A black boulder stands.

Beyond the black boulder
Is a waterhole near the path.
Beyond the watering places
Are boundary lines to the left and right.

Beyond the boundary lines,
Climb to "Flat Place."
After that, go forward.
A place called Jodugeri is beautiful.

Beyond Jodugeri lies the glittering tank.
Beside the tank lies the village Podur.
The people here live and act
As if they were very good people.

Leaving the tank,
Go forward to Attinatha village.
Here good people of peaceful nature
Are serving in the temple.

After Attinatha, climb higher.
Come to Sivapur, truth's home.
Beyond Sivapur lies
The Shining Throne of truth.

After writing this poem and several others, Elephant's unofficial poet laureate had to purchase a gun to defend himself from his victims, for one part of the poem is an attack upon the poet's enemies. This tangled epic is also a description of the things in Elephant's environment. Fields and forests, irrigation tanks and watering places, villages and towns, landlords and chieftains, and, above corrupt town and gritty village, the Shining Throne.

Through the poet's eye we see the environment and the region not as a defined area with the village in the center but as a trail leading upward from dishonest townsmen to fearless but victimized villagers to good-seeming people to actually good people, and finally to the Shining Throne. In its innermost meaning the poem is about the body of God and the movement of the individual upward through many rebirths until he reaches the Shining Throne.

The central structural perception of the South Indian world is just this, a massive unity of unlike parts working together in harmony. Although the parts that make up this great unity may be quite different, they also replicate each other in some ways. There are many kinds of people, but each person's body resembles the bodies of all other persons. Families, houses, villages—every kind of place or social unit—can be interpreted as analogous to the human body and to the body of God. However different or unrelated or even opposed things may seem to be, they are all essentially the same, and all contribute importantly to the harmonious functioning of the inclusive unity known as God, Paramahatma, Krishna, Shiva, and Brahm.

In answering questions about the kinds of things that exist, people in Namhalli make a sharp distinction between the natural and supernatural worlds. The natural world is divided into ground, mountains, forests, hills, oceans, and villages, whereas the supernatual world is divided into separate religious places, such as the loci of Brahm, Shiva, Krishna, and the Earth. Earth as a supernatural place is distinguished from earth as a natural place. Each of the natural and supernatural places, particularly those regarded as on the earth, contains beings, plants, and objects. Things in the sky, such as the sun, the moon, and the planets, are described as lifeless.

Forests and wildernesses contain wild plants, wild people, and wild animals—tigers, lions, foxes, boars, and monkeys. Mountains are the same as forests, except that they also contain stones. Bodies of water contain fish, snakes, and other aquatic creatures. A village consists of houses, men, cattle, and plants. When asked to classify kinds of men, most people throw up their hands in disgust. More specific questions elicit lists of kinds of jatis, kinds of workers, and kinds of relatives. Animals are listed in hierarchical order: first cattle, then lions and tigers, and finally dogs, goats, and sheep.

In sum, the universe consists of places, and each of these places may contain gods, men, animals, plants, and things in varying mixtures and proportions. All of the inhabitants and things in each location are arranged in hierarchical order. Each of the different items and locations in the universe contributes to its perfect functioning. All are tied together and interrelated by the pathways leading to the Shining Throne. The totality is beyond description or perfect understanding. Only a few may follow the way long enough and far enough to grasp the larger picture. Men live surrounded by beauty and divine perfection, but they see it not.

The people are wicked. The lotus will grow beautifully in muddy water. Its fragrance is known only to the bee. It will come and take honey from the flower. Just underneath the flower, there is the crocodile. It cannot understand the smell of the flower or its uses. Like that, the crooked people of this place cannot understand the value of wisdom even though they see every day such wise people as you. [From an old man in Elephant]

Where the European deity exists outside the Universe, playing with it like a toy, the South Indian deity *is* the Universe and more. The deity and all other things in the Heavens and on the Earth are subject to the Law. The Law, underlying the perfect and orderly functioning of all things, is *dharma*. Because dharma is the fundamental concept underlying both Hinduism and Buddhism, it is subject to many interpretations and has been given many meanings in English. Much that we might mean by law, right action, harmony, charity, truth, goodness, and virtue is included within the concept.

The notion of the perfect ordering of all things leads naturally to the question, "Why are things in such a mess?" The answer generally given begins with an analogy between the Universe and the human body: a healthy human body is fatigued at times and contains unclean substances; health is maintained by decay; perfection arises from disorder. In the same way, *adharma,* or negative dharma, is necessary to perfection. What is not-dharma is in some larger sense an aspect of dharma. Evil in the streets of Tamarind or among the corrupt officials of Elephant appears to be adharma. But because it is part of some larger and perhaps poorly understood aspect of universal perfect function, it might well be, had we but the wit to perceive it thus, dharma.

Following the same kind of argument, it can be seen that all of the creatures and things in the Universe possess a rough equality. All human beings may reach the Shining Throne. All things contribute to the functioning of the Universe. As with human beings, so with all other things: some are closer to the Shining Throne than others. Thus, ranks of jatis reflect spiritual progress in former lifetimes. Priestly Brahmans and Jangamas (Lingayat priests) are to be respected and obeyed because of their accomplishments in previous incarnations. Birth into a particular jati reflects reward or punishment for conduct in previous lives. A sinful Brahman is likely to be reborn as a particularly low form of life, but for as long as he is a Brahman, he is entitled to function as a Brahman and to be obeyed, particularly in religious matters, by those below him.

After many false starts, the individual works close to the Shining Throne. To reach the Shining Throne is to achieve a state called *moksha,* or *nirvana. Moksha* is not a state of union with God because the individual is already a part of God. It is a state of understanding that permits the individual to transcend the cares of everyday life, a state of release or separation. It is enlightenment. Because the achievement of moksha is an effort extending over many cycles of birth and rebirth, few persons, perhaps only Gandhiji (Mahatma Gandhi) in this century, reach a state approaching moksha. Those who seek moksha or who are on the verge of achieving it may come from any jati and either sex. For the most part, such persons live on fruits and nuts, wandering from place to place or establishing themselves in isolated parts of the forest.

Because far more persons claim to be saints than can be saints, rural people are skeptical about such claims. Saints (*sannyasis*) attempt to demonstrate their ability to rise above earthly things by abstaining from sex, deserting their families, and sometimes performing self-mutilation. A hermit living at an isolated shrine near Gopalpur was pooh-poohed as "unable to get along with his wife." When an internationally famous saint from Bombay was arrested as a charlatan by the Mysore police, the people of Namhalli were delighted; even so, they left his picture hanging on their walls. However, a woman near Gopalpur who lived on air and water, a feat mentioned in the ancient Sanskrit scriptures, was regarded as a genuine saint.

The difficulty that most people encounter in approaching moksha, or for that matter any very sophisticated spiritual understanding, results from a failure to see beyond the appearances of things and from the excessive adharma in the present-day world. Failure to perceive truth is caused by *maya* (illusion). Maya, sometimes personalized as a kind of malign force, refers to distortions of sense impressions stemming from involvement in the material world. As water glittering on the beach resembles silver, so sense impressions present falsehood as truth. A person who seees through the illusions caused by sense impressions may become a guru, or religious teacher.

> Oh, son, hear the great qualities of a Guru:
> He is free of the Desires.
> He can control sexual and other impulses.
> He can control his mind and make decisions.
> He can cut off the Desires when they secretly creep into him.
> Such a soul is a Guru.
> [From Namhalli, attributed to a Jain guru]

In the present epoch, *Kali Yuga*, the naturally deceptive qualities of sense impressions are augmented because the Universe itself is in one of its periodic states of disorder. During Kali Yuga, the son disobeys the father, the student disobeys the teacher, the servants disobey the master, the wife disobeys the husband. The people are wicked; disease and famine stalk the land. Taken together, the concepts of maya and Kali Yuga account for the presence of imperfection in a perfect universe. They serve to explain why so few individuals achieve the Shining Throne. What is needed now is a means—like Hope in Pandora's box—by which men committed to the sinful world of maya may yet perceive dharma and achieve moksha.

There was severe drought in Elephant in 1953, and water sources became polluted. Many people were too sick and feeble to plant their crops. The explanation:

> It is due to our karma. In our previous life, when someone asked us for a drink of water, we must have told him that we had no water or food to give. Now, in this life, we are suffering without water or food.

The man deceived by maya commits sins—*papagalu* or *karma*. When his lifetime has been completed, Yama (Death) sends his messengers. If the dying man is spiritually strong, he may wrestle with them until Yama himself comes riding on a water buffalo and drags him to Yamaloka (Yama's place). There, Dharmarayya (oldest of the five Pandava brothers and god of justice, or dharma) weighs the man's good and bad deeds on a scale:

> After death, a man or woman is born again. The man who commits karma [sins] is reborn in his next generation as a pig. The man who commits many sins will be reborn as a donkey. He who kicks others will be reborn as an ant and kicked.
>
> The man who does dharma will be reborn as the son of a king. If the king's son does dharma, he will be reborn as an educated man. A woman who does dharma is reborn as a virtuous woman and in her next rebirth becomes an angel in Heaven. [From an informant in Elephant]

There is a sense in which dharma and karma may be treated as opposed concepts: right action versus wrong action. But karma is also fate, written on the forehead when good and bad deeds are weighed in the balance. A person's karma determines the jati to which he will belong and the kinds of misfortunes (or rather, punishments) to which he will be subjected. In the sense that karma determines an individual's social role, it also determines his social duties. When people follow their social duties (obey their karma), when the son obeys the father, when the student obeys the teacher, the result is dharma. Far from being the opposite of dharma, karma provides the dynamic means of resolving discrepancies between the world of illusion and the perfect universe of dharma.

Despite the karma, or sin, which causes a man to be born again and again into the world of maya, there are a variety of ways of avoiding sin and securing progressively more favorable rebirths.

Although the pathways to the Shining Throne are diverse, and many may be followed at one time, the four major roads to Heaven are saintliness; *bhakti*, or unswerving faith; dharma, or right action; and karma, in the sense of dutiful performance. The Namhalli schoolmaster explains saintliness with the following poem:

> When my husband went to war,
> He sealed the doors with wax.
> But I became the mother of six children
> After removing the seal and the wax.
> I have my house full of children,
> Yet I had no union with my husband,
> Nor did I sow any grain, nor any paddy,
> Nor did I eat cooked rice
> Made from the paddy grown in the field.
> Oh, fathers and brothers who are going to war,
> When you see my husband there,
> Tell him I have gone with my lover. [1952]

The wife, enslaved and then deserted by her militarist husband, gains control of her six senses (taste, touch, hearing, sight, smell, and pain), turns away from the material world, and departs with her lover, God.

To control the six senses is to cease to feel pain or joy or other false illusions stemming from maya. In the rural community, those who have experienced great loss or sorrow, more specifically, old people who have no further responsibilities, are encouraged to follow the path of saintliness. In Namhalli in particular, it is common for old men to retire to their gardens to spend their last years in solitude and contemplation. The ordinary man or woman, with responsibilities to children and spouse, is discouraged from following such a course and criticized if he undertakes it.

Bhakti, or salvation through faith, is described in the following story:

A *rishi* (saint) and his wife were unable to have children. They worshiped Shiva for many years. Finally, Shiva asked them if they would like to have a truthful and honest son who would live for sixteen years or a dishonest son who would live for one hundred years. They replied that they wanted only the first.

The son who was born to them was truthful. He engaged continually in worship of his guru, his parents, and Lord Shiva. On the boy's sixteenth birthday, as he was worshiping Shiva, Yama came to him and began to drag his life out of his body. The boy embraced the *lingam* (symbol of Shiva). Shiva emerged from the lingam and ordered Yama to leave and stop bothering his son. Trembling with fear, Yama fled.

Shiva told the boy, Markandayya, that he had blessed him with a life of one million years. Markandayya told Shiva that he wanted to go away with him immediately. Finally, Shiva blessed Markandayya with a lifetime of nine million years. [From an informant in Namhalli]

Here, the simple, earnest devotion of the buffalo-like country bumpkin to any kind of God or religious principle is sufficient to guarantee spiritual progress. Valmiki, author of the *Ramayana*, won permission to write his famous biography after Rama carelessly suggested that he repeat endlessly, "Rama, Rama, . . ." Centuries later, when Rama came across Valmiki still repeating his name, he had no option but to endorse Valmiki as his official biographer. In Namhalli, the story is told of a lowly Leatherworker who was a devotee of one of the goddesses. When he went to her temple, the Brahman priests denied him admission on the grounds that he would pollute the sacred precincts. Crushed, the Leatherworker went into the fields behind the temple and began to pray. Suddenly, the wall of the temple fell away and the image of the goddess turned so that he could see it. Bhakti, or love of God, may be accompanied by prayer, worship, ritual, sacrifice, or self-denial, but the essence of bhakti is a deep and personal attachment to a particular deity.

The road of dharma is illustrated in the following tale:

Dharma and Karma were two brothers. Dharma, the older brother, was poor. He went each day to the forest and gathered wood for sale. His wife worked in the house, keeping it clean, bathing, and worshiping Shiva and Parvati.

Dharma and his wife never sat down to a meal without serving at least one poor and pious man or woman. Even though they had no children, they were happy and content. They had complete faith in Shiva and Parvati. They remembered them while they worked, and they constantly reminded each other that their good and bad actions were being recorded. They were following their karma and leading their lives in dharma.

The younger brother was the rich man of the village. He had a huge mansion and many servants. He loaned thousands of rupees and collected a heavy rate of interest. The hours of the day and night did not give him enough time for his work. He did not give a single copper to the poor or a handful of grain to a beggar. His wife was another miser.

She was always scolding the servants—that was her worship. No festivals
or ceremonies were celebrated in their house. They had no children.
They had wealth and all the necessities of life, but their house was not
happy.

One day Parvati asked Shiva why he was giving all the pleasures of
the world to the younger brother and all the troubles in the world to the
older brother. Shiva asked Parvati to come with him to the older brother's
house and test his dharma. In the guise of an elderly couple, they came
to Dharma's house. Dharma's wife was happy to see them and invited
them to enter the house and rest. When Dharma returned from the
forest, Shiva told him that he could not eat unless he first took a bath.
Shiva instructed the wife to bathe her husband with boiling water,
putting a quantity of chili paste on his head. Since both were devotees
of Shiva, nothing happened to them. Shiva and Parvati returned to
Heaven, and Dharma began to acquire wealth, prosperity, and children.

The younger brother became miserable when he saw his brother's
improved condition. His wife learned that her in-laws had become prosperous after bathing in boiling water and chili paste. She poured boiling
water on her husband's head, and he died. The wife died a few days
later.

At Yama's place, their karma and their dharma were recited to Yama
and his judgment was delivered. They were to be placed in a well filled
with human excrement and nibbled by worms. When Dharma and his
wife died, Yama himself carried them to his palace. They were given
seats in Yama's palace and treated to all of the heavenly pleasures.
[From an informant in Elephant]

Dharma and his wife, like most people, followed a number of
pathways to Heaven, but the crucial factor in their spiritual success
was generosity. In Elephant, dharma means charity—gifts to temples, kindness to animals, food for the poor, gentle treatment of a
bullock retired from agricultural chores, water or buttermilk to a
thirsty stranger. In Namhalli, Gopalpur, and other more sophisticated places, dharma refers to any kind of good deed, while *dana*,
or gift-giving, refers to charity.

A person of low spiritual attainments is capable of recognizing
dharma expressed as charity but may be incapable of recognizing
dharma in other situations. This is a common theme in folklore and
literature and is best illustrated by the episode in the *Mahabharata*
in which Dharmarayya (the oldest of five brothers and the god of
dharma) gives away his kingdom and the brother's communal wife
in a gambling game rather than break his word, even though he
knows his opopnent is cheating. Dharmarayya's brothers, being

younger and lacking his understanding of dharma, are incensed by his action. In the end, they cannot bring themselves to disobey their older brother and all five brothers go into exile. The common theme of all such "dharma stories" is that understanding dharma is beyond the capacities of the ordinary person. It is a bit much to give away one's wife and kingdom in a crooked card game, particularly when you know it's crooked; and it takes a rare devotee to bathe in boiling water as a demonstration of faith. But if the way of dharma is too rocky for most people, the way of karma, or obedient action, is open to all.

In the *Bhagavad Gita,* Arjuna and Krishna discuss a coming battle. Rather than participate in war, Arjuna wishes to live as a hermit in the woods. Krishna argues that Arjuna was born into a warrior jati and that it is his duty to fight. Krishna gives Arjuna a glimpse of his true all-encompassing form. Arjuna sees that the immorality of war is illusion (maya) and accepts his part in it. In the same way, each of the jatis making up a rural community has its role to play in the smooth operation of the community and the Universe. Beyond jati, each social role has appropriate duties: wife must obey husband, daughter must obey father, younger brother must obey older brother, impure jati must obey pure jati, those born as Farmers must farm, Shepherds must keep sheep, Blacksmiths must work at the forge, Leatherworkers must make sandals and eat beef, and Brahmans must pray for the benefit of the world.

In Namhalli in 1953, poor rainfall and a consequent lack of employment made it difficult for the Leatherworkers to obtain food. An epidemic spread among the village cattle. The Leatherworkers purchased a diseased bullock and slaughtered it in daylight in a small ravine behind the village. Because "all the gods live in the cow," cattle-killing, like Brahman-killing, is a sin far worse than ordinary murder. Hearing about the slaughter of the bullock, a leader of the mutton-and-pork-eating Shepherd jati spoke out: "Because of this sin, your people will not get to Heaven." The Leatherworkers replied, "Without eating beef, we could not have survived; just as God has made you people to eat mutton, so he has made our people to eat beef. In the end, everyone gets to Heaven."

Karma, the path of duty, guarantees that those who commit the sins inevitable when the conduct of life is governed by mere sense impressions will nonetheless get to Heaven. The great cycles of rebirth and of spiritual promotion and demotion now become relevant to everyday concerns. Man's best chance of salvation lies in the meritorious fulfillment of his assigned tasks. As each jati fulfills its function, or karma, the village acquires dharma. All things go well; the people are happy. Rain falls on time and in the proper quantity. There is no illness. Human beings are born into ranked jatis each having its own karma. All other things in the Universe—plants, animals, deities, planets, worlds—are also arranged in a spiritual hierarchy. Because it is Kali Yuga (a sinful age) and because mere men cannot be expected to understand these things fully, there need not be any great agreement about the ranking or function of things in the Universe. Still, everyone believes that all things in the Universe are ranked and that this ranking parallels the ranking of the different jatis.

High gods, the deities who play important roles in Sanskrit literature, are associated with high-ranking and vegetarian jatis. Their temple images must be served by Brahman or Lingayat priests. The highest deities, Shiva and Parvati, Vishnu and Lakshmi, or Brahm and Sarasvati, are the special concern of the high-ranking jatis. The Lingayat Farmers of Elephant and Namhalli worship Basavanna, the white bullock who serves as the vehicle of Shiva and who came to the earth in human form to establish the Lingayat religion. Those who were converted gave up meat eating and agreed to dine with—but not to intermarry with—all other Lingayats. The Jangama, or priestly Lingayats, claim to be the descendants of Brahman converts and therefore holier than all other Brahmans. The Brahmans claim that the Jangamas were not descended from Brahmans or else that they sacrificed their Brahmanic rank by taking food from non-Brahman Lingayats.

The rough-and-ready meat-eating farmers of Gopalpur attach most importance to rough-and-ready deities like Hanumantha, Rama's monkey-faced helper, or Bhimarayya, the bumptious, demon-descended Pandava brother. Lower-ranking pork-and-beef-eating jatis tend to worship the meat-eating and sometimes terrifying mother goddesses. These goddesses, said to be forms of Shiva's consort, Parvati, are assigned the task of chastising humanity when "sin is up." They do so by bringing epidemic diseases, such as smallpox and cholera. Although there is a possibility that the disease goddesses represent an earlier, "pre-Hindu" form of religion, they fit completely into the modern pattern of jati and religion. If there are meat-eating people, there must be meat-eating deities to serve them.

Animals are also ranked in the spiritual hierarchy. Cattle, who serve as the home of the gods and also give milk and pull plows, stand highest. Monkeys, horses, eagles, and other animals having special relationships to the deities stand next. Sheep, goats, and other useful animals occupy an intermediate rank. Donkeys, pigs, dogs, and cats are low in rank. When people are asked to list animals, they generally list them in the above order. It follows that cowherds rank higher than shepherds and that the Washerman, who uses a donkey to carry blood-defiled menstrual garments to the pond, ranks low. Each item in a village (or in any other locale) fills a dharmic function. If beings or things are out of their proper order, or if they fail to perform their proper function, dharma is violated and divine retribution follows. The life of the South Indian villager can be seen as a progression along a pathway leading from one locale or one stage of development to the next. At each locale or stage, he takes his proper place in the hierarchy of relationships and, if he is to continue his progression, he performs the actions he believes to be appropriate and according to dharma. To the extent that the villager is ignorant of dharma, and he often regards himself as such, his actions cannot be according to dharma. But where dharma is violated unknowingly or as part of the duty (karma) of a particular jati, the individual may still expect to gain spiritual reward. .

One consequence of this view of the Universe as a planned whole whose essential nature includes both wrong and right action is that the mistreatment of other people and of the environment can sometimes be rationalized as in the service of a higher good. A man who has stolen land from others may say, "I have committed a lot of sins in my life, but I had to do it for the benefit of my family." For most people—for the Washerman as he beats his donkey, for the master as he beats his servant—there is always the chastening thought of role reversal in future rebirths. Donkey, servant, Washerman, and master are all equals before the law of dharma. Although people do what they must to each other and to the world around them, a feeling of sympathy and kinship underlies every human relationship and is often given expression in doctrines of nonviolence and respect for life.

Although concepts like dharma, karma, maya, Kali Yuga, and moksha can be interpreted as ways of understanding the environment and man's place within it, the precise impact of such grand ideas on human behavior is difficult to evaluate. The strongest and most obvious impact is in the area of human relationships. People everywhere in South India see themselves as representatives of ranked jatis, each of which contributes to the community through the fulfillment of its karmic tasks. The members of any particular community arrange for the distribution of work and wealth within it in terms of the models provided by the South Indian world view. Individuals, households, and communities are regarded as tiny replicas of the Universe and are considered to be governed by the same principles of dharma and karma. All that is necessary for the smooth operation of any social entity is that its different parts carry out their functions in accordance with dharma.

The social structure of a household, community, or kingdom is strengthened by the fact that obedience, even to a bad or evil master, is an act of great virtue. For those at the bottom of the hierarchy of jatis, it is no small consolation to consider the possibility that in the next life the roles of master and servant may be exchanged. The worse the master and the better the servant, the greater the likelihood that such an exchange will take place. For the couple unable to raise children, for the farmer unable to raise a crop, for anyone confronted with misfortune or oppression, there is always the thought, often expressed, that such misfortune is a well-deserved punishment for sins committed in a previous life.

In terms of ecological relationships, the South Indian world view provides a major impetus for the establishment of systematic and organized patterns of interaction with the environment. Each environment is conceived as having its own dharma, its own special requirements. Once that dharma is discovered and applied the pattern established is likely to be maintained indefinitely. Western observers, considering the supposedly fatalistic South Indian belief that events in the universe are predetermined and the apparent rigidity involved in the maintenance of a fixed, traditional set of right actions with regard to every aspect of the environment, have often felt that the South Indian world view makes flexible change and adaptation difficult or unlikely.

There are, however, flexibilities within the concept of right action. First, different places and situations and different kinds of men have different karma and different interpretations of dharma, leading to a choice among acceptable solutions to particular problems. Second, because this is Kali Yuga, there is uncertainty about the precise nature of dharma within any given context. Right action can always be reinterpreted, and it is precisely the high man in the spiritual, political, or educational hierarchy who is charged with defining and redefining dharma. Third, a great deal of confusion and ignorance is anticipated, for even if there were one and only one correct answer to a particular problem, humble people may not expect to attain it. For example, tradition in Namhalli asserts that the earth is a flat object resting on the backs of elephants. Most of the people in Namhalli would agree that this is the case. At the same time, all of them have learned from the schoolmaster that the earth is a round object spinning in space. They know that this is so because when the manager of the telephone factory calls New York, it is dark there. In South Indian thought, such a patent contradiction is resolved in terms of the doctrine of maya, the same thing wearing many different guises.

In the use of new medical or agricultural techniques, the same principle of open-mindedness holds. People are always glad to add a new technique to those they already use. The new idea need not drive out the old: it may merely supplement it. In other fields, where patterns of right action are strongly established, change is likely to be resisted. The farmer who understands how to grow millet is likely to reject minor improvements, particularly since these come from educated persons who therefore "know nothing" about farming. The suggestion that a farmer does not know the dharma of his daily activity verges on insult. A revolutionary new crop or a completely new system of farming appears to be much more acceptable. People in Namhalli consider themselves to be the world's foremost experts on millet growing, and here, except for a few obvious improvements, such as the substitution of a steel plow for a wooden plow, there has been little change in long-established patterns.

People in Namhalli are more willing to experiment with the rice crop, probably because it is a relatively new crop and they are therefore willing to acknowledge that there may be some things they don't know about it. The use of transplantation, chemical fertilizers, and insecticides on the rice crop has been labeled "the Japanese method." This labeling suggests that there is an alternative and equally dharmic way of growing the crop. A completely new crop, such as tomatoes or grapes, stimulates the farmer to investigate and discover as much as possible concerning its dharma.

Innovation that changes the relationships of things in the environment or that prevents people from filling their proper role in the community is not dharmic. Therefore, when the government built railroads, it became responsible for the welfare of the Lambadis, whose traditional occupation had been the transportation of salt and other goods from place to place. Handloom weavers, who faced starvation as early as 1800 due to the competition of imported textiles, are still supported by special taxes on machine-made cloth.

On the whole, the South Indian view of life appears to be more ecologically or systems oriented than the traditional Western view. If an innovation fails to take into account the preexisting interrelationships of gods, people, animals, plants, and things within a particular place and situation, it will lack dharma and will therefore fail to work well. The Western insistence upon consistency ("There is only one straight road") and upon unique and linear causation ("Because of a nail, the shoe was lost . . .") may not in fact be especially realistic.

Within the framework of its master concepts, the South Indian world view provides detailed instructions concerning almost every aspect of relationships among human beings and between human beings and the environment. There is a proper or right way for almost everything to be, and there is a proper or right way to act in almost every situation. These ideal patterns are discussed in detail in the following chapters, because every aspect of South Indian village ecology is founded in an interaction between ideal, or dharmic, patterns specified in the world view and the unique environmental circumstances in which each community finds itself.

VARIATION

Although the South Indian world view can be seen as a steady force which ensures that the social and environmental relationships characteristic of each community are derived from the same master plan, the master plan itself is often modified in particular villages.

In Elephant, religion centers very largely on sin and punishment.

This is dharma: We must give charity to others because we might have taken a loan in a previous life; now we return that loan in the form of dharma. Making wells and irrigation tanks, removing stones and making a path, protecting the poor from abuse, giving clothing to the poor, taking an injured animal from the forest to the village to help it, planting trees, and so on, are all dharma.

Sin is harming poor people. If a man refuses to give water for irrigation or for drinking, steals when others are sleeping, cuts plants that provide shade for animals and people, kills cattle or injures them, keeps out the poor and invites the rich, obstructs those who wish to make dharma, or abuses people who can't talk and beats those who have no hands, that is sin.

Even Elephant's Svamiji, a man schooled in the religious literature, speaks little of hierarchy or of the karma of different jatis. Similarly, there is little talk of maya or moksha and little debate concerning the fine points of religion.

Compared to other villages, Elephant is remarkably uncomplicated. The village itself is small, and its nearest neighbors are too distant for frequent interaction. On the topic of dharma, no voice contradicts that of Svamiji. Because Elephant is a small community containing only one jati, there are few complexities in human relationships, and the rules of life can be spelled out in simple and direct fashion. There really is no sin in Elephant. Theft and violent conflict are literally unknown except as they are visited upon the community by voracious outsiders.

Lacking close neighbors or a strongly differentiated social system, Elephant tends to emphasize dealings with the natural environment.

In Gopalpur and Namhalli, life is seen as more complex and is strongly characterized by interpersonal relationships. Both villages comprise a variety of jatis, and both are located in highly developed plains regions where they are in constant interaction with the residents of other villages and towns. Not surprisingly, religious stories told in Gopalpur and Namhalli emphasize the difficulties involved in determining the nature of right action. In Gopalpur, a popular ballad tells of a woman who must choose between seduction by an evil railway conductor and having her child pulled to pieces before her eyes. Being a virtuous woman, she sacrifices her child. In Elephant it is easy to avoid sin; in Gopalpur it is very difficult.

In Gopalpur, where most of the population is illiterate, people pride themselves on being rough farmers lacking any taste for religious subtleties. This attitude probably reflects the traditional character of the Gopalpur region and the vast gulf between the educated rich and the working poor. Traveling minstrels and many kinds of religious specialists transmit abundant and complicated perspectives of the world, but there is little tendency to debate alternative viewpoints or to adopt any pathway other than that of duty and hard work.

In Namhalli, as a result of education and urban influence, there is a much greater tendency to debate the finer points of Hindu doctrine, such as the extent to which concepts of form can be applied to the deity, the evidence for the existence of Jesus,* the justification for the inequality of the lowest jatis, and the possibility of worshiping the deity without using rituals or ritual paraphernalia. The reflective mode in Namhalli is not due entirely to urban influence, for the older men of the village have always had the option of retiring to their gardens to live out the remainder of their lives in saintly contemplation. Here, the existence of gardens as places that need watching and also as places where it is good to be seems to have led to the development of personalities adapted to solitude, contemplation, and, ultimately, the pursuit of saintliness.

---

*Residents of Namhalli claim to have confounded Mr. King, a Christian missionary, when they pointed to the sun and said: "There is our god, now show us yours."

Chapter 2

VILLAGE PLANS AND STRUCTURES

Like the rules of a game, the South Indian world view provides the individual with information about the field on which he is to play out his life, the objects of his actions, and the various strategies he may use in his long journey to the Shining Throne. In addition to the general strategies of life outlined in the preceding chapter, the world view provides a detailed plan for the construction of a proper sort of village and for the establishment of patterns of relationships with other human beings. This chapter deals with the various structures and relationships that must be developed before the game of life actually gets under way. It describes the game's setting, structures, and equipment; provides a roster of the participants; names the positions they will occupy; and states what roles they will play at the outset.

Although the world view informs the members of a village about the way things ought to be—how the land is to be defined and what things should be on it, how people should dress and how they should relate to other people—the design of any particular village often represents a compromise between the cultural ideal and the materials at hand. Just as in sandlot football it is often impossible to construct a playing field of the proper dimensions, so in the design of a village it is often impossible to fulfill all the requirements specified by the cultural tradition. As the people in each village wrestle with the particular problems posed by their environment, they must modify the grand design. In some ways each village comes to resemble all other villages, but in others each is unique. Let us now consider the structures and patterns characteristic of the village of Elephant.

Elephant is situated on a hilltop and surrounded by lands that have been set aside as a forest preserve. Its boundaries are defined not by the boundaries of other villages but by the boundaries of the reserved forest. Due to poor management and the ruthless depredations of timber merchants, the forest surrounding Elephant consists of thorny scrub, perforated here and there by towering trees that have somehow survived the woodman's ax. Because people graze their cattle, acquire the right to harvest certain fruit trees, and gather firewood in the forest, the effective village boundaries extend some distance beyond the limits of the cultivated fields that define the village lands. Where the forest ends, stone walls and thorn fences mark the lands. Inside the walls and fences is a domesticated world within which terraced fields march neatly up the hillside, and every piece of land and every tree and bush reflects the impress of the farmer's hand. During the rainy season each terraced field is a tiny work of art, bordered by the yellow flowers of niger, shaded by mango and tamarind trees, and carpeted with millet, mustard, and castor bean.

Halfway up the hillside, where a brook sometimes flows, tile-roofed houses are strung out casually along twisting trails. More or less in the center of the cluster of houses making up the village stands a large mud-brick building erected to house pilgrims who may one day come in unnumbered thousands to bring wealth and fame to Elephant. So far, the pilgrimage center, or mathe, stands empty. Not far from it is the village temple, a rectangular building containing the fenced-off shrine of the village deities and open at the eastern end. Here ceremonies and meetings take place; here weary travelers spread their blankets.

At the northern end of the village an earthen barrier forms a pond where cattle and sometimes clothing may be washed and from which water may be drawn to irrigate small gardens of chili and eggplant. At the southern end of the village a grotto shaded by flowering trees contains two shallow wells with stone staircases leading into them. The upper well is for drinking water, and the lower well is for bathing. Within and below the village a number of deeper wells have been constructed in the hope of finding a perennial supply of water. So far, only one new well, constructed

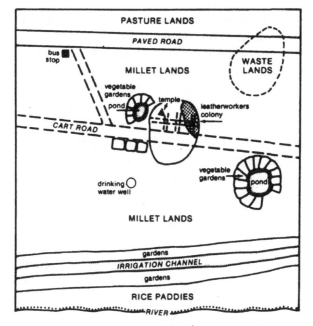

Figure 3

far below the village, gives promise of providing water in the dry season. Heretofore, people had to bring water from a distant stream, and sometimes they were forced by drought to leave the village with their cattle.

Elephant's position in the reserved forest, its hilltop environment, and its difficulties in obtaining water all combine to give a unique character to its fields and buildings. Although many villages in South India contain patches of forest and wasteland, most are located on relatively flat terrain. Their fields are rectangular and require no terracing; their boundaries are defined by the boundaries of other villages. Lacking flat and well-watered lowland areas, Elephant also lacks rice lands and irrigated gardens.

Elsewhere in South India, villages are laid out so as to provide a rich selection of land types. The fields of Namhalli, for example, form a narrow rectangle reaching from the bottom of a river valley to the top of a rise. Rice is grown on the flatlands near the river and below an irrigation channel. Gardens irrigated by shallow wells and containing a profusion of orchard and vegetable crops line the irrigation channel. The village proper is situated about a half mile from the garden strip, surrounded by fields of rain-fed millet crops.

The village is high enough to escape the swarming mosquitoes of the bottomlands, but low enough so that its wells reach down to water. Near the top of the ridge are wastelands and pasturelands.

Gopalpur, by contrast, stands beside a perennial stream, and its fields encompass a selection of sandy soil suitable for summer (rainy season) crops, loamy soil suitable for fall crops, and irrigated soil suitable for rice crops. Houses in Gopalpur and Namhalli are laid out in relatively straight rows. Being somewhat larger than Elephant, both Gopalpur and Namhalli contain temples and more numerous shrines for minor deities. They also contain small shops where cigarettes, matches, betel leaf, and other necessities of life are sold. Namhalli, as befits a modern village, possesses streetlights and a school building.

Although there are a few places in South India where houses are scattered about the fields rather than concentrated in a "nucleated" village, the general pattern is one of tightly clustered houses surrounded by a patchwork of fields. Because they are surrounded by trees and constructed of such earth materials as stone and mud, most South Indian villages seem closely integrated with the land.

Houses in Elephant consist of a small rectangular room separated by clay storage jars into a cooking area and a living area. At night, husband and wife sleep on the kitchen floor while the children sleep on the floor of the living area. In the morning, each person rolls up his bedding and stores it in a bamboo attic beneath the eaves. Most houses have walls of compressed mud and tile roofs; a few have walls of mud-smeared mats and roofs of thatch. Household furnishings consist of "god pictures" hanging on the walls, an unvented fireplace, a grindstone, and a mortar for pounding rice. In the kitchen a flat stone slab serves as a sink for washing dishes and as a bathing place. Utilitarian pottery is used for cooking and storage. Cattle are kept in fenced enclosures outside the house.

In Namhalli, traditional houses were built of mud brick with tile roofs. In the past, they often took the form of rooms that enclosed a courtyard where cattle were kept. As the village has modernized, cement floors have replaced the traditional dirt floor plastered with cowdung. Living rooms now contain chairs and small radios. Often the kitchen stove is equipped with a chimney, the walls are plastered and whitewashed, and the family valuables are housed in a steel safe or trunk. For protection from bandits and the summer heat, houses in Gopalpur are walled with stone and roofed with branches and leaves surmounted by a foot-thick layer of clay. There are few windows in the walls, and light filters through tiny openings in the roof. As in Namhalli, the rooms enclose a courtyard occupied by cattle.

Throughout South India, then, village houses reflect the available materials and special features of the environment. Small one- or two-room houses, often with thatched roofs, provide shelter for small or poor families, while large houses with courtyards shelter extended families consisting of several generations. Rich people may have even larger houses, often several stories high and reflecting urban patterns of design.

In Elephant, women wear a sari—a single long piece of cloth—and a blouse. The sari is wrapped around the waist, and one end is brought across the breasts, behind the neck, and over the head. Most men wear a small piece of cloth tucked between the legs and supported by a silver waistcord; a sleeveless shirt; and a towel or shawl slung over a shoulder or wrapped around the head. Wealthier men wear shirts with sleeves and collars, short trousers, and a long strip of white cloth that is wrapped around the waist. Most men also possess woolen blankets and leather sandals. Men wear silver boxes around the neck to signify their membership in the Lingayat religious sect; small earrings and rings or bracelets. Women also wear rings and earrings, and all married women wear a piece of gold suspended from a cord around the neck. Glass bangles, nose jewels, and a wide variety of other jewelry are also worn.

The heavy use of jewelry by both men and women, saris for women, and turban or headcloth, shirt, and wraparound waistcloth for men—this is the general pattern of dress throughout South India. The ability to raise or lower the sari or waistcloth and to remove shirts or headcloths provides a means of adapting to daily and seasonal changes in temperature. Within this general pattern of dress, great local variation occurs. There are innumerable ways of wearing a sari, a waistcloth, or a headcloth. Shorts or a cloth passed between the legs may replace the waistcloth, and the headcloth may be a long, heavy sheet or a short towel. All of these garments are made in different colors and in different weights and qualities of cloth. Modern clothing, long pants with shoes and socks, has modified local dress in many regions, but a person's clothing still tends to reflect his place of origin and his social standing (though not, as a rule, his jati).

SOCIAL STRUCTURE

So far, the village has been discussed in terms of land, housing, and dress. These things reflect the specific structures that people have imposed on the environment in their pursuit of food, clothing, and shelter. But a village contains another, intangible kind of structure—a social structure. This consists of patterns of relationship among persons that establish the part each is to play in the relationships between the village and its environment. Let us now examine the kinds of people who farm the lands, live in the houses, and wear the clothing.

The basic unit of South Indian social structure is a household composed of a husband, a wife, and their children. Ideally and according to dharma, the female children marry and go off to live in their husbands' houses at puberty or earlier. The male children marry and continue to live in their own house along with their wives and children. Within the household, all members share in the work of the family and all male members are regarded as co-owners of the family property. When the father, or perhaps the grandfather, dies, his role as headman of the family descends to his oldest son, and the family members continue to work and eat together as a single unit.

In real life, demographic, economic, and political factors often make it impossible to maintain such a jointly owned extended family household. Many couples have no children, or the children they do have are female. People who have no property or whose holdings are small simply cannot support a large family, and their sons leave home shortly after marriage. Conflict develops between fathers and sons or among brothers. Such conflict is often believed to be triggered by disagreements between mothers-in-law and daughters-in-law or between the wives of different brothers. In many cases, large families are held together not so much by their own sense of unity as by the unremitting hostility of their neighbors, and it is not unusual to find large households at the center of the disputes that sometimes disrupt the normal functioning of the village.

In a "poor" village like Elephant, which contains no really wealthy families and has a high rate of divorce and infant mortality, most of the households are nuclear families consisting only of a married couple and their young children. Such households are often augmented by the husband's widowed mother or by other single relatives of the wife or husband. Sometimes these small households are depleted by death or divorce; often the wife is too young to have children, the couple is barren, or the children fall victim to childhood diseases. The nuclear family, although recognized as the ideal type in both the local world view and the mind of the anthropologist observer, is an ideal that is often unrealized.

Where things do proceed according to dharma, the nuclear household possesses a unit of land sufficient to meet its grain and cash needs. Such a unit of land—a "plow"—represents the acreage that a single household can conveniently cultivate. Within the family, the husband and the older male children carry out the bulk of the farm work, while the wife and the older female children manage the household. Although bringing water from the well, grinding millet, pounding rice, and preparing meals require substantial amounts of time, women are also expected to help out in the fields, especially in such duties as harvesting greens, transplanting seedlings, and weeding. Although the South Indian world view stresses the subservience of women and urges them to worship their husbands as their gods, the close cooperation and functional interdependence of the members of a nuclear family tend to create a situation that is often indistinguishable from equality. This is particularly true in poor families where the wife contributes substantially to the family income.

Where close family relationships are threatened by adultery or by a refusal to perform traditionally assigned tasks, conflict often results. Although such conflict normally takes the form of wife-beating or child-beating, husbands and fathers may themselves be subjected to verbal abuse and, where physical strength permits, to beating. The world view of South India posits a family ideal that can be realized only by those who are successful in fathering male children and in maintaining a level of wealth and power of which the subservience of female to male and younger to older is practicable and enforceable. But the existence in practically every village of well-managed and efficiently operating households is sufficient to keep the family ideal alive and to act as a strong incentive toward the practice of dharma in day-to-day family relationships. The ideal patterns provide models when a family quarrel must be adjudicated by a committee (*panchayat*) of male neighbors or elders. The son who beats his father and the wife who beats her husband are likely to be regarded unfavorably by such a committee.

The formation and future history of a nuclear family is critically dependent on the process of selecting a hardworking and virtuous wife. Among wealthier families the characteristic strategy is to select a bride between the age of 6 and 12 from a relatively poor family and a distant place. Such a bride is often much younger than the bridegroom, completely cut off from her own family, and raised by her mother-in-law. This type of marriage tends to delay the birth of children until the husband is well over thirty and thus to put off the time at which he might want to set up a separate family of his own. The time at which the bride might enter into successful conflict with her mother-in-law is similarly delayed.

A more common strategy, employed by those of average income, is to select the daughter of a close relative, such as a mother's brother's daughter, a sister's daughter, or a father's sister's daughter. Here the bride may well be from the same village as the groom and, although almost always younger, closer in age to him. Such a bride tends to be relatively well treated by the bridegroom's parents, and the resulting marriage more nearly approximates the kind of partnership characteristic of many small South Indian families.

One of the reasons for observing every propriety in the arrangement of marriages is that an improperly chosen bride might serve polluted food and so endanger the health and spiritual well-being of the groom and his family. Because the gods do not smile on incestuous or otherwise improper marriages (any marriage with a lineal relative of the father, no matter how distant, is incestuous), multiple misfortunes, and especially childlessness, may follow upon the improper selection of a bride. Marriage to a close relative is regarded as a certain means of avoiding incest because the bride demonstrably belongs to a lineage with which safe and successful marriages can be contracted.

Among some groups in South India, notably the Nayar of Kerala, the purity of the family is preserved by keeping both men and women in their original households and by reducing the status of the husband to that of a casual visitor. Here, traditionally, the operating family consists essentially of brothers and sisters, and property passes from the mother's brother to the sister's son. Although the Nayar system of residence and inheritance seems quite different from the more typical pattern, it can be regarded as an intense expression of the need to preserve the household from the contaminating effects of strange women and, perhaps more important, to ensure that the family property is kept in the family.

The ideal of the large extended family household has important implications for the interpretation of other aspects of village structure. Brothers are hierarchically arranged in terms of age and, like jatis, they often perform different functions. The oldest brother may assign duties to other members of the family and advise them concerning dharma, while the younger brothers may handle different aspects of the family economy, one tending the garden, another herding cattle, and still another caring for the family dry lands. All of the brothers form a council whose decisions deeply influence the conduct of the family head. The hierarchical arrangement of brothers, the division of functions among them, and the balance of power between a headman and a council are characteristic of many other aspects of village organization. Very often the village itself is considered to be a variety of undivided joint family in which the different jatis represent a team of brothers and the headman and accountant represent the father and mother.

When a large family divides into its component nuclear families, the result is an array of independent units, all of which are descended from a single male ancestor. Although the component families no longer share food cooked on a common hearth and usually do not continue to farm their lands jointly, the oldest brother or the father tends to retain an important position as the senior representative of the different units. The children of brothers continue to be regarded as siblings because they share common descent from the same ancestor. Future generations descended in the male line from the original ancestor will also be regarded as

brothers and sisters with whom marital arrangements are incestuous. Although some groups in South India trace descent in the
female line, the most common pattern involves the establishment
of patrilineages in which descent is traced in the male line and
marriage with lineage brothers or sisters is forbidden.

As male members of a lineage migrate to other villages, the lineage becomes an organization that cuts across village boundaries.
Because single jatis are often represented by only a few households
in each village, it follows that a particular jati in a particular village often consists of a single lineage. Under these circumstances,
the senior male—the older son of an older son—becomes the headman of the lineage and jati within the village. In Namhalli, such a
headman represents the jati on the village council and participates
in negotiations concerning the jati's position in the hierarchy and
its economic and ritual responsibilities in the village. The headman
also represents his segment of the lineage in a council composed
of lineage representatives from different villages. Very often the
senior male of the entire lineage is a headman who represents all
the segments of his lineage on a jati council.

Where a jati in a single village is large, it often contains representatives of more than one lineage. Typically, representatives of
other lineages are brought into the village when a nuclear family
without sons brings in a daughter's husband to care for the family
property. Usually such an imported lineage is regarded as junior
to the already established lineage, and the headman of the established lineage serves as the headman for all the lineages within the
village.

In different parts of South India, the size and social importance
of lineages are highly variable. In Namhalli and Elephant, lineages
possess religious shrines to which their members make occasional
pilgrimages and at which the entire lineage gathers periodically
to conduct major ceremonies. In Gopalpur, lineage religious shrines
are less important, lineage headmen are hard to identify, and lineage membership often means little more than the possession of an
adihesaru, or family name. Brahmans and representatives of other
high-ranking jatis are organized into *gotras,* or clans, which are of
enormous size and represent the descendants of a small number of
original ancestors. Throughout South India, the lineage serves to
create a sizable body of persons who are regarded as brothers and
sisters and therefore cannot marry each other. Because particular

lineages may include most of the members of any particular jati in a village, and because marriage must take place within the jati, the existence of lineages guarantees that many marriages take place between rather than within villages. In contrast to northern India, marriages within the village are not forbidden and are often regarded as ideal.

The term *jati* means "type" or "species." Marriage between jatis can take place if it follows an established precedent. In Namhalli, members of the Pancala, or Artisan jati, marry members of the Lingayat Artisan jati under the justification that previous similar marriages have been successful. The unwitting commission of brother-sister incest is prevented by the fact that the biological relationships between the two jatis are known. In Gopalpur, when a member of the Christian jati contracted a marriage with a girl from another jati, both abandoned membership in their original jatis and affiliated themselves with the Ayra Samaj, a religious sect that rejects the jati concept and encourages marriage between jatis. Because South Indians strongly prefer to marry persons who are known to be relatives, the issue of marriage between jatis rarely arises. The bride may not belong to the same lineage as the groom but must belong to a lineage that has previously had marital relationships with the groom's lineage. Marriage into a strange lineage or into another jati could well turn out to involve a distant sort of brother-sister incest.

Although it is generally useful to define jatis as groups that do not intermarry, the group within which intermarriage actually takes place usually need not comprise the entire jati and may in some cases comprise members of different jatis. The jati may be defined not only in terms of marriage but also in terms of specialized dietary practices, ritual obligations, occupations, or religions. In fact, any class or group of people having distinctive customs or practices may be labeled a jati. In terms of world view, each jati is thought of as having a distinctive role in social life, and the perfect functioning of a village, region, or nation arises in the fulfillment of such roles. In the South Indian view, unity arises out of the proper relationship of distinctive parts rather than out of the elimination of the differences among them. Until recently, for example, the assimilation and Americanization of ethnic groups in the United States was considered to be desirable, and the preservation of unique languages and customs was regarded as divisive.

Although similar assimilationist fantasies are by no means absent in South India, the major thrust of South Indian thought is that the preservation of unique jati practices is essential to the proper functioning of the social system. In South India, "out of many, one" becomes "one is many."

The village order is seen as the outcome of the working together of different jatis, and the dharma, or perfect functioning of the village, is believed to result from a situation in which each jati performs its own special karma, or duty. Although most of the jatis in a particular village may engage in agriculture, each jati, especially if its representatives are regarded as permanent residents, possesses specific occupations and ritual obligations that can be performed by members of other jatis only when persons in the legitimate jati are unavailable.

This ideal picture of a village has somewhat the same status as the ideal picture of a joint family—it cannot always be realized in practice. Small villages and hamlets, such as Elephant, often comprise only one or two jatis. Such communities rely on larger neighboring communities for the services of specialized jatis or do without. Larger communities, such as Gopalpur or Namhalli, each containing over a hundred households, attempt to attract migrants from specialized jatis, but a full range of services can be obtained only in villages containing several hundred households.

The economic interdependence of jatis may be expressed in terms of direct payments for services in cash or grain or in terms of jajmani relationships. *Jajmani* is a North Indian word that has come into common usage in the absence of any generally used South Indian equivalent. Basically, a jajmani relationship is a contractual relationship in which members of different jatis exchange services or provide services in exchange for a regular annual payment of grain and other foodstuffs. A member of the Barber jati obtains the services of members of the Blacksmith, Carpenter, and Washerman jatis by agreeing to cut their hair. Members of farming households obtain the services of such specialized jatis by providing an agreed-upon payment at harvesttime. When a farmer threshes his grain crop, each of the specialists who serve him comes to the threshing ground and receives a measured portion of the grain. The exact amount paid is determined in part by the traditional position of each specialist in the hierarchy, but it may also be negotiated. Thus, if members of the Barber jati decide that the traditional payment is too small, they may refuse to provide services until it is increased, and until such a labor dispute is settled, no member of the jati will cut hair. In effect, the jati forms a region-wide trade union, and all barbers within the region charge the same price. When the Barbers demand more than members of other jatis are willing to pay, the resulting conflict tends to be decided in terms of dharma by political or religious figures of region-wide importance.

The right to be served by a particular member of a service jati and the right to provide services to a particular household are inherited. In Namhalli, where Barbers, Washermen and Blacksmiths have all found lucrative factory jobs, each specialist must either serve his clients on weekends or find other specialists to provide the required services. Although a particular household may cease to use the services of any Washerman or Barber, it is awkward and difficult to shift from one to another. Such a shift almost always involves litigation, in which the householder must demonstrate incompetence or dishonesty on the part of the person entitled to serve his family.

Because Namhalli is located near towns where barbering, laundering, and many other services are available for cash, it is possible for its households to dispense with traditional economic services. On the other hand, each of the specialist jatis provides ritual services that cannot be obtained in urban shops. For example, the Washerman—and only the Washerman—provides the clean saris on which the bride and groom must walk during their wedding ceremony. It is possible to conduct a marriage ceremony only if the household has maintained harmonious relationships with its Washerman and with all the other jati representatives who provide essential ritual services. Even where jatis do not provide mutual economic services, they are likely to provide essential ritual services. In Gopalpur, for example, the Shepherds, Farmers, and Saltmakers are all farming jatis which do not exchange economic services on any regular basis, but they all possess crucial roles in the conduct of ritual.

In strictly economic terms, a village consists primarily of farmers engaged in direct competition. The divisive effects of such competition are reduced and in some cases eliminated by the fact that each household is economically dependent on other households from specialist jatis and ritually dependent on households from each of the important jatis in the village. In effect, the myth that makes multijati villages possible is the myth that the survival and proper functioning of any one jati is dependent on the survival and proper functioning of every other.

Because different jatis commit different kinds of sins in performing their duties, it follows that some jatis are higher or purer than others. The Brahman and Jangama jatis practice vegetarianism and carry out important priestly and religious duties, and their members claim to be higher or purer than members of other jatis. In consequence, Brahmans do not take boiled food, which might be impure, from members of other jatis. The Jangamas belong to the Lingayat religious sect, which was founded about A.D. 1100 and spread across Mysore State and other parts of South India by a process of conversion and baptism. All members of the sect, regardless of their original jati rank, are expected to practice vegetarianism and to take food from each other. The Brahmans claim to be "higher" than the Jangama because the Jangama take food from "lower" jatis, while the Jangama claim to be higher than the Brahmans because they were originally Brahmans and now follow "correct," or dharmic, religious practices. The Pancala, or Artisan jatis, said to be composed of blacksmiths, goldsmiths, carpenters, stonemasons and temple builders, claim to be directly descended from the deity Visvakarma and therefore to rank as high as Brahmans.

Although members of any of these three vegetarian jatis may be temporarily compelled to occupy a lower position in the hierarchy than that to which they feel themselves entitled, they do so only under protest. Here again, the concept of jatis as forming a neat and orderly hierarchy along a dimension of ritual purity represents an ideal that is not fully realized in practice. Differences of opinion about the proper ranking of jatis are generally attributed to the fact that this is the time of Kali Yuga, when "sin is up" and the divine order is in temporary disarray.

Although vegetarian jatis may disagree about their proper place in the ritual order, there is little disagreement with the idea that all vegetarian jatis are higher than all nonvegetarian jatis. What disagreement exists generally takes the form of arguing that the members of a particular vegetarian jati secretly eat chicken and therefore are not entitled to the rank they claim. Members of some vegetarian jatis do in fact eat fish and regard it as a vegetable.

Members of high-ranking nonvegetarian jatis, sometimes referred to as "clean" jatis, usually eat fowl, fish, and sheep or goat mutton. In Namhalli, members of clean jatis eat pork, but in Gopalpur, perhaps because of Muslim influence, pork is regarded as unclean. Members of the vegetarian Lingayat Farmer jati are generally ranked higher than members of the clean nonvegetarian jatis, but the difference is often regarded, except by the Lingayats, as very small. Many of the clean jatis are also Farmer jatis having large populations and substantial political influence. Thus, the ranking of the clean jatis varies greatly from one place to another, and where there are several in a village, there is often controversy about their relative position in the hierarchy. Muslims, who eat beef but not pork, may claim to be outside the hierarchy altogether and therefore superior to everyone else. In Namhalli, Muslims are usually said to rank below the clean jatis, though not to their faces, while in Gopalpur, Muslims, especially priestly Muslims, are considered to rank as high as the clean jatis.

Below the clean jatis are a series of jatis that consume pork or other meats considered unclean and that practice such unclean occupations as washerman or barber. The unclean jatis usually contain small numbers of people, and many are migratory. Below all of these are the A.D.'s, or "Aboriginal Dravidians." Members of these jatis eat beef and engage in such traditional occupations as street sweeping, leatherworking, or scavenging. Basically, there are five major classes of jatis—priestly, vegetarian, clean, unclean, and polluted. These classes are generally arranged in a clearly defined hierarchy, but within each class the relative position of the different jatis is often open to debate.

Although many authors have interpreted this ritual hierarchy in terms of economic status or social prestige, there is great variation in the extent to which position in the hierarchy affects wealth or social position. Members of the vegetarian and clean meat-eating jatis, including Muslims, labor under few economic or social restrictions, and they may include large landloards and other members of the rural aristocracy. In any given region, Brahmans and members of numerically large clean jatis are more likely to be wealthy. On the other hand, birth into a high-ranking jati is no guarantee of wealth, and it is acknowledged that misfortune or loss of wealth may be the inevitable result of sins committed in a previous life. In most places a Brahman who gives birth to many daughters and few sons may find himself impoverished as a result of expenses incurred in arranging his daughter's marriages. Brahman marriages, unlike those of most other jatis, typically involve the payment of large sums of money to the bridegroom or his family. In the Gopalpur region a constellation of factors, including high dowry payments, serve to limit the size of Brahman families and to ensure that Brahman males commence family life with a substantial cash bonus.

The bulk of the population of rural South India consists of members of clean farming and specialist jatis who own small amounts of land and are able to maintain their families at or slightly above the subsistence level. Members of almost any jati can attain such a level, but it is relatively difficult for members of low-ranking jatis to do so. Landless laborers find it difficult to acquire the education, equipment and capital needed to enter the yeoman class. Members of low-ranking jatis, such as the A.D.'s or the Stoneworkers, are likely to be charged exorbitant rates of interest or otherwise swindled out of economic gains which others evidently regard as "ill-gotten." In some parts of South India, beatings, thefts, house burnings, and other forms of violence administered to members of low ranking jatis by those of higher rank make economic mobility virtually impossible. For many landless laborers, especially those of the A.D. jatis, economic mobility has recently been facilitated through conversion to Christian and other religious sects, which provide a new jati definition (a different karma), or through government and urban employment. In Namhalli, with its long history of urban contacts, many individual members of low-ranking jatis have made substantial economic progress; one has been a member of the state legislature.

Although the hierarchy of jatis is important in a variety of contexts, it is sensible to view social and economic ranking in South Indian villages primarily in terms of distinctions among landlords, small farmer-craftsmen, and landless laborers. Small numbers of people belonging to wandering or begging jatis might be ranked below the landless laborers. The landless laborers usually live in crudely constructed thatch-roofed houses; they possess little property beyond the ragged clothing on their backs; and their family size is restricted by malnutrition and high infant mortality. The aristocrats of the group are such specialized jatis as Stoneworker or Toddy Tapper, those who tap palm trees to produce beer, whose members draw a somewhat higher wage than farm laborers.

Yeoman farmers and craftsmen generally have more substantial houses; they purchase new clothing two or three times a year, sometimes have substantial savings, and are able to borrow money. Relatively prosperous yeomen may be able to afford a servant, and most yeomen can afford some degree of conspicuous expenditure—for weddings and funerals in such traditional settings as Gopalpur; for bicycles, wristwatches, and visits to the cinema in such modern settings as Namhalli. The economic position of the yeomen varies considerably from region to region. In Namhalli, where they have access to factory employment or to the substantial profits of vegetable and fruit production, their level of living is relatively high. In Elephant, which was until recently a relatively impoverished community, yeoman farmers possess relatively poor housing and have very little cash income beyond that required for survival.

Membership in the landlord class generally involves the possession of several hundred acres of good land (or 10 to 20 acres of rice or garden land); a large and well-constructed house; and sufficient income to permit the purchase of mechanized equipment, the sponsoring of lavish ceremonies at which the entire village may be fed, or the educational support of all male offspring through the B.A. degree. Representatives of this class are absent or scarce in the less productive agricultural regions. Large landlords are not found in the rocky hills surrounding Elephant and are concentrated around irrigated lands in the Namhalli region. In both regions, members of the yeoman class are politically dominant. In the Gopalpur region, with its large concentrations of fertile and irrigated lands, landlords are numerous and politically dominant.

The organization of any particular village depends on the kinds of jatis and classes that are present as well as on its unique local ecology. Because Elephant consists almost entirely of the members of a single jati and a single class, village decisions tend to be made by a panchayat which is essentially an assembly of all the adult males and many of the women and children. Several of the wealthier men lay claim to such formal titles as "village head" or "village landlord," and thereby acquire the somewhat costly privilege of entertaining visiting government officials and the sometimes remunerative privilege of helping to collect taxes. Elephant also possesses a Lingayat priest, or Svamiji, who plays an active role in the adjudication of disputes and who organizes and supervises the ceremonial life of the community.

Namhalli has a formally organized panchayat consisting of a senior male, or headman, drawn from each of the major jatis in the community, including the low-ranking Leatherworkers. Village officials consist of a government-supported Headman, an Accountant who lives elsewhere, and a Watchman drawn from the Leatherworker jati. The Headman is from the Jangama jati, while the Accountant is a Brahman. Here, as in Elephant, the village officials deal with visiting government officials and collect taxes. One hundred years ago, the Namhalli Headman was a powerful and authoritative figure drawn from the landlord class. More recently, the Headman has been a relatively powerless figure, and in 1952, when he attempted to exert his traditional authority, he was replaced with a Headman drawn from the Shepherd jati. Periodic attempts by the state government to replace the traditional village organization with its own salaried officials and with an elected panchayat have resulted in the gradual erosion of formal political mechanisms and their replacement by an informal village council consisting of relatively wealthy small farmers and a well-organized group of factory laborers and schoolteachers.

Until recently, Gopalpur was dominated by a single powerful member of the landlord class and by such village elders as this Headman might choose to summon when the occasion seemed to call for a council meeting. With the decline of the economic fortunes of the Gopalpur Headman, the yeoman farmers have developed ties with wealthy men in other villages. This process may have accentuated the development of political factions. At any rate, the decline of the Gopalpur Headman has gone hand in hand with increasing disputation and disorder within the village. By government reckoning, Gopalpur is too small to have an elected panchayat of its own and has therefore been merged for administrative purposes with a neighboring village. At present, power seems to rest with four members of an elected panchayat which theoretically governs both villages.

Ideally, then—and Gopalpur and Namhalli approach the ideal—a village is a ranked set of jatis, each of which is composed of ranked lineages and households. Where things are according to dharma, the different jatis each contribute their unique and divinely assigned talents to the smooth ritual and economic functioning of the entire community under the direction of an official leadership. Although the ideal is seldom completely realized in practice, the overall arrangement of individuals in families, lineages, and jatis, in groups of patrons and clients, and in groups of neighbors and friends provides the teams of individuals whose activities establish and maintain the ecological relationships characteristic of the South Indian village.

In terms of both dharma and economic reality, the primary ecological relationships of the South Indian village involve the agricultural activities by means of which it supports itself. The following two chapters consider the varieties of man-land relationships that constitute the agricultural subsystem of the overall village ecology.

Chapter 3

AGRICULTURAL TECHNOLOGY

The karma of the rural community is raising food crops. The farmer often sees himself as a practical man unaware of theological and intellectual subtleties, yet he never doubts his importance in the scheme of things: "One man must plow so that twenty may eat." Although not all members of the community belong to jatis whose primary social responsibility is agriculture, almost every resident in a rural village is a farmer of farm laborer as well as a practitioner of a traditional occupation.

Rainfall, soil, seasons, temperatures, and other aspects of the environment that affect the raising of agricultural crops are crucial to the fulfillment of the village's sacred purposes. The farmer, the man who manages (even if he does not directly own) particular plots of land, must select plants and agricultural techniques that will permit him to reap a profitable harvest. If the soil is poor and the harvests are small, the village may be isolated from other villages and communities because it lacks the capital required to entertain visistors, attract and manipulate government officials, and draw tradesmen and entertainers.

To survive, a village must produce enough crops to support its population, build up a stockpile against bad years, and satisfy such needs as the purchase of clothing and the payment of taxes. The maintenance of village populations, elaborate systems of social stratification, and complicated ceremonial patterns depends on the quantity of agricultural production. In choosing particular techniques to exploit available resources, the members of the village commit themselves to particular activities: cattle must be fed and watered daily, and crops must be harvested within a few days after they ripen.

The application of agricultural technologies to village lands involves subtle and complex interactions not only within the village but also between the village and neighboring communities, government agencies, and supernatural beings. To simplify matters, this chapter emphasizes the technology that is applied directly in grain farming, animal husbandry, and fruit and vegetable production. Although these three basic technologies are closely related, the most significant involves the production of the grains ragi (*Eleusine coracana*), jolla (*Sorghum vulgare*), and rice.

Ragi. The least productive of the three major grain crops is *ragi*, a small, red-seeded millet that can be grown in poor soil and without much water. Ordinarily, ragi is grown on the sandy soils of hills, ridges, and valley sides. In the rich dampness of bottomlands, ragi is likely to turn white and die. Given drainage and a heavy rain soon after planting, it clings to life. Where lands are flat, systems of bunds (earthen barriers) and ditches are used to prevent excessive runoff and to guide the waters of a heavy rain around the fields. In Namhalli, where the slope of the land is relatively gentle, systems of ditches bring excess rainwater to ponds which are used later to irrigate small gardens of eggplant, chili, and potatoes. Level fields require little preparation beyond clearing brush and timber from the lands.

In Elephant, ragi fields are expensive to prepare because they require terracing. In 1952, 300 rupees and a year's food supply for a family of stoneworkers were required to terrace one acre. Considering that the value of a ragi field ready for cultivation was often less than 300 rupees per acre, terracing the lands of Elephant seems to represent a poor investment, but the alternative would be to move to another village, away from relatives and friends. For the most part, ragi land is worth little, costs little to create, and produces little. There is a resulting simplicity of social and economic arrangements: Elephant consists almost entirely of members of a single jati and has economic relationships with relatively few specialized jatis from other villages.

In Elephant and Namhalli, the beginning of the new year (*Ugadi*) is marked by the purchase of new clothing, the whitewashing of houses and the spreading of fresh cowdung on the floor and in the street in front of the house. Hunting expeditions or gambling games, conducted in memory of the time when the oldest of the Pandava brothers gambled away his kingdom in a dishonest game, help to determine whether the farmer will be lucky in the coming year. For many farmers, the months ahead are lean. The slender grain supplies left from last year's harvest are exhausted, and grain for sowing must be borrowed from a wealthy neighbor. Each sack borrowed must be paid back twofold at harvesttime.

According to the South Indian world view, *Ugadi* marks the beginning of "the rains." Each rain lasts for two weeks, according to the phases of the moon, and is supposed to have specific properties. During one rain, hard thundershowers may be expected; during another, a drizzle. Normally (when it is not Kali Yuga and people are not committing manifold sins), the rains come on time and what falls is just right for the growing ragi crop. Religious worship at Ugadi and throughout the agricultural season is directed at purification of the worshipers and appeasement of the deities in the hope that memory of the worshipers' many sins will be forgotten and that there will be dharma and good rains.

Starting before Ugadi, the men, women, and children of Elephant carry 70-pound baskets of manure up the steep hillsides to their rocky fields until each is spotted at 10- or 12-foot intervals with little heaps of manure. In Gopalpur and Namhalli, manure is carried to the fields in carts, permitting a larger expanse of lands to be farmed productively. Situated on the side of tall, ocean-facing hills and inhabited by persons of great religiosity, Elephant usually enjoys good rains. Due to the slope of the lands, following rains some fields are dry enough to plow while others are too muddy. Groups of friends and relatives come together, four or five men plowing one man's field, then another's. In 1952, when half of Elephant's population was sick as a result of drinking polluted water, the fields were plowed collectively by those healthy enough to do so.

Because Basavanna, the founder of the Lingayat sect who came to earth first as a white bullock and later as a man, forbids yoking bullocks to the plow on Mondays, the followers of Basavanna in Elephant and other villages begin their plowing at the dawn of any day but Monday. For the first plowing, the field owner brings what he can afford, most often coconuts, betel leaves, areca nuts, sandal sticks, camphor, flowers, turmeric, saffron, sandal paste, sacred cowdung ash, puffed rice, and brown sugar. The plowman decorates his plow and, facing to the east, worships it. The coconut is broken, and the assembled family members and friends circle the oxen and the plow three times. Foods and other articles that have been offered in worship are then distributed to the children and adults.

The ideal for every plowman is possession of a matched pair of bullocks, pure white like Basavanna and of enormous size and strength. Such a pair is expensive and consumes only the best fodder. Brass horn covers, bells, and other ornaments required to display a beautiful bullock properly are also expensive. The average farmer reluctantly settles on a small and scrubby pair of bullocks that will eat little and work hard. The neck of the bullock must bend downward to accommodate the yoke of the plow, and if there is no natural depression an attempt is made to deform the neck of the calf. Calves are castrated with knife and cautery while still quite young. The yoke is a round pole laid across the necks of a pair of bullocks, which must therefore be of approximately equal height. Wooden pegs inserted into the pole keep the bullocks in position and provide a means of fastening the rope running around their necks. A pole attached to the plow is tied to the center of the yoke. The plow itself resembles the earliest known form of plow, but now instead of a single crooked branch there is a separate pole, blade, post, and handle. The blade of the plow has an iron tip. Steered with one hand, the plow does not turn the soil but makes a channel some three to six inches deep. A moldboard plow of the lightweight variety available in South India today requires greater exertion on the part of man and bullocks, but it plows twice as fast. Moldboard plows based on an American pattern were first introduced to South India in the 1920s by Methodist missionaries and are now probably used by more than half the plowmen of South India.

The first furrow is generally made by a senior member of the family which owns the field, the actual plowing often being completed by an adolescent boy. Initially the field is plowed in an east-west direction, one man or boy generally plowing about half an acre per day. Plowing is usually done in the mornings and evenings, roughly from 6:00 to 10:00 A.M. and from 3:00 to 7:00 P.M. After the next rain, generally the second of the season, the fields are plowed in a north-south direction. The time required to plow and variation caused by the condition of different soils following a rain limit the number of acres that a single plowman can handle. The optimum pattern seems to be to have several fields in different locations or with different types of soil so that the period of plowing can be stretched out as long as possible following a rain. By using these devices or by having each field plowed by a team of plowmen, a farm family can handle a somewhat larger acreage than would be the case if a single plowman cared for a single field in a single location. Scattered fields also provide insurance against failure of the crop in a single field due to too much or too little rain. In a dry year, farmers in Elephant may lose their crops in sandy soil or well-drained locations. In a wet year, crops may be lost in heavy or poorly drained soil.

Following the first two plowings of the field, additional manure may be brought and any stubble remaining from last year's crop removed and burned. A third and fourth plowing is now required to ensure that the manure is thoroughly mixed with the soil and that all clods are broken up. If the soil is soft, a rake may be substituted for the plow; very often the rake will be used after the fourth plowing. Using a trowel, women remove stubborn weeds from the edges of the field and feed them to the bullocks.

Now, in expectation of heavy rainfall, seed must be sown as quickly as possible. In Elephant, seed is generally broadcast, probably because of the rocky nature of the soil; elsewhere a seed drill is used. After ragi is broadcast, furrows are plowed about four feet apart in the field and such intercrops as *avare* (a kind of bean), *jolla*, and castor bean are planted in the furrows. Often, niger (*Guizotia abyssinica*), an oilseed, is sown around the circumference of the field.

After sowing, the field is raked and smoothed with a branch. Because sowing should immediately precede heavy rainfall, it must be accomplished as quickly as possible. For this reason, sowing is usually done by teams of men, and the farmer has to recruit relatives and friends to assist him at sowing time. The accompanying table indicates the sources of labor available to ten Elephant farmers during the 1952–53 season. Because a large number of fields in any one village must be sown at the same time, a single village, such as Elephant, must have a means of importing temporary labor. At sowing time, laborers are not usually hired for cash. Individual farmers do not wish to entrust anything as critical as sowing to hirelings, and cash or surplus grain to pay laborers is in short supply. For Elephant, then, somewhat more than half the laborers who come for sowing are related to the farmer through his wife or his sisters and are therefore likely to be living in other villages.

Table 1. Those Who Help with Sowing

Household No.	Patrilineal	Wife's Relatives	Sister's Relatives	Friends
1		1	2	
2	1	2	2	
3	1		1	1
4	1			2
5	1	2		
6			3	
7			3	
8				3
9	1		2	
10	3	1		
Total	8	6	13	6

Sowing takes place 2½ to 3 months after the first rain of the season. If this fell on April 15, sowing would take place at the end of June, just when the drizzling monsoon rains were beginning. The crop is thinned by running a cultivator over the field from north to south two weeks after sowing, and from east to west a week later. This operation is unnecessary in places like Gopalpur, where ragi is transplanted rather than sown, due to the absence of April and May showers. Two to four weeks after the Elephant crop has been thinned, depending upon rainfall and weed growth, the field must be weeded. It takes 15 laborers about five days to weed a five-acre field.

Here again, the requirements of the crop must be reflected in social arrangements. The labor resources of the farmer, his family, and his friends and relatives are insufficient to provide a team large enough to weed a field in a reasonable length of time:

If you own five acres, four or five laborers are needed in addition to household members. In my case, I don't employ any laborers unless I must be away from the village at the time of weeding and harvesting. To get labor, what I do is start ten days before harvest working in other people's field. When the day comes, there will be ten people available for cutting my crop. If only five people come, due to rain or some other circumstance, the other five will pay me cash for the days I worked. [From Elephant]

If a man is fortunate enough to have cash at weeding time, he may hire laborers directly. At harvesttime he can pay his laborers directly in grain, but if he is poor it is more practical to exchange free labor. Laborers utilized in transplanting, weeding, and harvesting are paid in labor, grain, or cash. They are likely to prefer grain to cash payments because they would receive less grain if they purchased it from a middleman than if they obtained it directly from the farmer.

After weeding has been finished and before the harvest is begun, there is little work. In Namhalli, cattle are turned loose in the fields to graze, forcing the plants to send up more heads and delaying the harvest. In addition, special efforts are made to fatten cattle for sale, though in Elephant cattle are generally not sold each year and are therefore not fattened. As the grain ripens, the lean months come slowly to an end. Fruits, vegetables, and forest products stimulated by the rains become increasingly available, and unripened grain is roasted and eaten.

At harvest time, the farmer's situation shifts from one of abject poverty and hunger to one of relative wealth and plenty. On each field, the harvest proper is generally accomplished in five or six days by 20 laborers. The laborers work with sickles, seizing a handful of grain stalks, sawing them off at ground level, and placing them to their rear as they work their way up the rows formed by jolla, bean, and castor plants. The harvest season places maximum stress on the manpower of the village, and even bringing in teams of laborers from nearby villages may not be sufficient to complete the harvest quickly and efficiently. The farmer works from dawn to dusk and sometimes, if there is a full moon, through the night. The cost of labor rises to meet the demand, but this is of little concern to the now affluent farmer.

After the grain is cut, it is placed in stacks near threshing grounds made by covering a flat area with cowdung plaster. In the morning grain stalks are spread out on the threshing floor to dry, and by afternoon two to four persons attack the stalks with long bamboo flails. Three men can thresh and winnow the produce of five acres in 15 days. On the last day, all the remaining straw is spread on the threshing ground and a dozen or more cattle are driven around and around over it to remove the last clinging seeds of grain. In Namhalli, grain is threshed with stone rollers.

The threshed grain is piled in a heap in the center of the threshing ground and decorated with fragrant flowers. Women and children draw pictures of agricultural implements on the ground. Coconuts and other offerings are brought, the decorated heap of grain is worshiped, and the offerings are distributed to the assembled crowd. After the ceremony, all persons who have claims on the farmer's grain come forward to take their share: the moneylender, the Headman, the Blacksmith, the Carpenter, the various priests, the schoolteacher, the Barber, the Washerman, and all the other village functionaries. Traditionally, the Headman was given a percentage of the grain representing the farmer's taxes. Nowadays, taxes are paid in cash and are based not on the farmer's yield but on the value of his land. Persons lacking formal claims on the farmer's grain are each given a small portion in charity. The farmer's affluence dwindles rapidly, but at the same time he builds up a stockpile of goodwill and dependence that will be useful in the coming year.

The remaining grain is placed in storage jars inside the farmer's house or buried in a pit in the village street. Through the year it will be used to make charitable contributions, purchase clothing and utensils, and feed the farmer's family. When the grain jars are empty, the farmer makes obeisance before his patron, moneylender, or Headman, and if he has behaved himself in the past he is loaned sufficient grain to last until harvesttime. Failing this, he and his family seek work in more prosperous lowland villages.

White Jolla. In the Gopalpur region and a few other parts of South India, there are large patches of deep black soil on which it is possible to raise a special variety of sorghum that is used as cattle fodder and to make a tortilla-like bread. Because the soil holds water over prolonged periods, two crops a year can often be obtained on these lands.

Because sorghum is a valuable cash crop that can be raised even when the rainfall is poor, these black soil lands are five to ten times as valuable as any other kind of unirrigated land. The farmer wishing to work such land must either serve as a tenant for someone else or borrow large sums of money in order to buy it. On other soils, the processes of plowing, thinning, transplanting, weeding, and cultivating are carried out much as they are for ragi. Sorghum harvesting is considerably simpler, however, because the plants are large, easy to cut, and can often be pulled out by the roots. The grain is carried on a fist-sized head which is cut off the stalk and thrown on the threshing ground. Bullocks are driven around the threshing ground until the large seeds are knocked off the heads. The large size of the grains makes winnowing comparatively simple.

Cucumbers, beans, and lentils of various kinds, and edible wild plants grow among the canes of sorghum so that, like the ragi fields, the sorghum fields provide a rounded diet for man and beast. Also like ragi, jolla is not so much a crop as a group of crops linked into an ecological system that includes men and cattle. Cow manure serves the jolla field as it serves the ragi field; the jolla provides cattle fodder, and the cattle provide milk; men provide labor, and the jolla provides bread. Without a human being present to tell us, it would be difficult to determine for whose benefit jolla, cattle, and people coexist.

Sorghum has a longer growing season than ragi because it can be grown through the fall and winter. This means that labor is in demand over long periods of time, and it becomes practical to maintain permanent laborers throughout the year. Traditional forms of slavery and peonage have declined over the past century or so, but wealthy farmers in India as in the United States will do almost anything to guarantee a labor supply.

The use of permanent laborers makes possible the cultivation of large acreages by a single farmer or by one farmer and his tenants. In the Gopalpur region, for example, there is an aristocratic class of landlords, most of whom own in excess of 200 acres. Small farmers raise ragi on sandy soils and utilize relatively small acreages of black soil. Very often the farmer's son works for a landlord to pay for his marriage or to pay off the debt incurred when the family lands were purchased.

Technologically, ragi and white jolla have similar requirements, but the ability of white jolla to grow during the fall and winter, while other crops grow during the summer, makes possible a two-crop economy. This facilitates the development of landless laborers and landed proprietors, a process which is not encouraged by ragi agriculture. Further, because the land used for white jolla is highly productive, it provides the economic basis for a more complex social system.

Rice. Rice agriculture, depending as it does in South India upon abundant water and complex schemes for its distribution, generally involves a large investment before the crop can be planted. Social stratification is merely a side effect of white jolla agriculture, but a complex division of labor seems indispensable for anything but the simplest kinds of rice agriculture. The man who constructs a paddy in a swampy corner of his ragi or jolla field does not need much help to get on with his farming, but where the development of rice lands requires elaborate dams and water distribution systems, many men are essential.

Rice agriculture involves the usual steps of plowing, sowing, and harvesting, but it requires more labor at every stage because everything grows faster in a rice paddy and because water control must be maintained constantly. If water supplies are truly abundant, two and three crops can be grown during the year. Given a reliable water source, rice is more productive and more dependable than either ragi or jolla. Ownership of a rice field guarantees an assured income so long as the necessary labor is expended. Where large acreages are devoted to rice, relatively little space is left for the small landholder. Wealthy landowners control large acreages which tenants and laborers farm for them. The very rich and the very poor come to dominate the scene. In Madras State and Kerala, where the largest classes are wealthy landowners and poverty-stricken laborers, something approaching class warfare occurs.

Garden and Orchard Crops. In Namhalli, a strip of land between the rice lands at the bottom of the valley and the ragi lands on the higher slopes has a water table from 5 to 30 feet high. Here it is possible to obtain water throughout the year. The result has been the planting of a variety of trees, bushes, and annuals in tiny, half-acre gardens.

Garden crops in Namhalli include sugarcane, betel leaves, areca nuts, coconuts, mulberry, ginger, coffee, cardamon, pepper, oranges, limes, mangoes, cauliflowers, cabbages, carrots, radishes, potatoes, sweet potatoes, chili, napier grass, flowers, tomatoes, grapes, cereals, and gourds. All of these crops have different cultural requirements, but in general, irrigated gardens require year-round labor and year-round protection. In these respects, garden agriculture resembles rice agriculture, in which two or three crops are produced each year. The central difference between the two is that rice requires much less protection on the part of the individual landowner.

Monkeys, small children, and thieves are a constant threat to fruit trees and vegetable crops, and even casual pilfering represents a considerable loss to the owner. Partly for this reason, there is a tendency for gardeners to live in their gardens. Carried to its logical extreme, this trend lead to the pattern typical of Kerala, where the farmers have ceased to live in settlements and live on individually owned plantations instead.

Garden agriculture, like rice agriculture, is dependable and provides a source of cash. Unlike the various forms of millet agriculture, garden and rice agriculture provide inadequate fodder for animals and men. Rice is more expensive and less nutritious than millet. The ideal situation from the farmer's viewpoint is one in which rice is exchanged in the market for one of the millets. Market exchange is even more necessary if garden crops are raised. One cannot live on betel leaves or coconuts alone. The farmer who depends on a garden crop is automatically involved in a cash economy, since he cannot consume more than a fraction of what he produces.

Animals. For the most part, South Indian crop production involves the use of bullocks for traction. Cows and female water buffalo not needed for milk production may also be used, and male water buffalo are often slaughtered and eaten by Muslims, Christians, and beef-eating Hindus. Unlike Mexican bullocks, Indian bullocks are castrated while quite young and treated as pets. They are therefore comparatively gentle and friendly. Bullocks are trained to recognize their names and to obey simple commands, so it is not unusual to hear a farmer shouting "Shiva, left" or "Basavanna, right."

Small, scrubby calves are usually selected for breeding purposes, and are bred to cows upon payment of a fee. In some places, male calves are dedicated to particular temples, after which they theoretically possess the freedom of the village. Such animals, lacking any definite owner and relatively uncared for, have a habit of disappearing mysteriously. Useless cattle do not survive very long in most villages. A faithful pair of bullocks may sometimes be allowed to survive long after they have ceased to be useful, but the common pattern is for the animals to be sold from person to person until they finally collapse in the field while pulling a poor man's plow. In four years spent in Mysore villages, I saw only two retired bullocks, both in Elephant, where fodder is cheap. I have never seen a retired cow or water buffalo.

Although it may seem churlish to deny an honorable retirement to an animal that has served long and hard as worker and family pet, the incidence of totally useless animals in South India is small except where fodder is abundant. My personal experience may have been selective, but a number of other indications suggest that slaughtering useless animals or working them to death is the common practice. First, no anthropologist who has lived for any length of time in any South Indian village has reported the presence of any significant number of useless cattle. Second, there are substantial numbers of Muslims and beef-eating Hindus in all regions. Third, there are beef markets in all major towns and cities of South India.

Reports in the anthropological literature of large numbers of economically useless cattle can easily be explained. Most of the observers knew little about livestock, and they may well have been unaware of the fact that Indian cattle are herded rather than penned and that individual animals often wander about freely before returning to their stalls. Cows used for plowing are useless as sources of milk and may therefore appear erroneously to be economically useless. South Indians, particularly those who are vegetarians, worship and love cattle and are therefore fond of pretending that no one eats them, even where the manifest evidence is otherwise. And it is the case that wealthy men often establish hostels for retired cows in order to earn *punya*, or merit, and these sentimental institutions are readily visible.

Bulls, cows, bullocks, calves, and water buffalo are vital elements in the economy of South India. The manure that keeps the fields fertile year after year comes from these animals. The milk of the cows and water buffalo is vital for the survival of children. Bullocks pull the plows, harrows, and rakes and tread the newly harvested grain. Cowdung mixed with water plasters the walls, floors, and streets, and fills the tiny holes in the baskets used to winnow and store grain. Cowdung fuels the blacksmith's forge and, where wood is scarce, the housewife's fire. Cattle urine is invaluable as a quick hand wash, a cure for various diseases, and a purifying (some say punitive) drink. The farmer's life and destiny depend on possession of a good pair of bullocks and a cow to provide his children's milk.

Next to cattle, sheep and goats* are the most important livestock. Sheep and goats are generally raised for meat, rarely for milk. The slaughter of sheep and goats often takes place at festivals and ceremonies, usually as a sacrifice to a nonvegetarian deity. Sheep are the special but not exclusive interest of the Shepherd jati. Members of this jati remove the wool and make it into coarse blankets that are used for warmth at night, for protection from the sun and rain, and for transporting grain and other materials. Formerly, Shepherds dressed in wool and carried staffs. Sheep and Shepherds tend to be most numerous where the countryside is rugged and unproductive and there are large acreages of wasteland.

Most families of meat-eating jatis try to keep a few chickens as a source of eggs and meat. Chickens generally run wild in the village, being locked up only at night. Pigs are raised by a relatively few members of very low-ranking jatis. Few villages are without pigs since their services are vital for the disposal of refuse. Particularly in Muslim-influenced areas, pork has 'very low status as a food, and many jatis that eat fish, fowl, and mutton do not eat pork.

In most villages, dogs and cats exist in a state of toleration. Cats are almost never regarded as pets; dogs usually have owners and sometimes, if there is local hunting, a cash value. Both animals are regarded as unclean and are rarely fed or handled. Often they are dread scourges, sneaking into the house, upsetting the milk container, or stealing the freshly cooked dinner.

Donkeys are the special preserve of the village Washerman and of those who transport salt and other materials in isolated regions. Horses, usually stunted ponies, are owned by storekeepers and landlords who must travel from place to place and are prepared to endure any agony rather than demean themselves by walking. Aristocratic ladies and invalids may be transported by bullock

---

*Goats have long been outlawed in Madras because of their destructive grazing habits.

cart. Ducks, geese, and peacocks appear occasionally, and social relationships, generally of a rather hostile kind, are maintained with monkeys, bedbugs, cockroaches, and lice. Wild birds infest most villages, are rarely molested, and are quite tame. Fish occur in rice paddies, tanks, and streams and are harvested periodically for personal use or sale.

Chapter 4

AGRICULTURAL ECOLOGY

A village is created when people move into unoccupied areas, construct houses, and prepare the land for agricultural use. The founders carry with them fundamental ideas about the nature of things drawn from the South Indian world view (Chapter 1), as well as the specific ideas and materials of agricultural technology (Chapter 3). As the founders attempt to actualize the technological and social relationships they believe to be appropriate, a dialogue is established between their culturally established dreams and ideals and the realities of the new environment. Out of this dialogue—out of successful and unsuccessful attempts to establish proper arrangements in a new place—there arises a new set of relationships between the community and its environment.

At the simplest level, the effect of these relationships is the capture of solar energy by agricultural plants and the distribution of this energy throughout the village and beyond the village to the wider society. The flow of energy through the village is by no means automatic. Resources taken from the fields must be returned if crop production is to be maintained on a continuing basis, and the energies of bullocks and human beings must be applied to the care and treatment of crops and the transportation of the harvest from the fields to the village and beyond.

Because the world view and the specifics of agricultural technology brought to the new location supply a broad outline of the means by which crops are to be grown and yields distributed, it is possible to speak in general terms of South Indian village ecology and to think of individual villages as representing an orderly replication of a way of life sanctioned and supported by the South Indian world view. Fundamental ecological relationships among cereal plants, cattle, and human beings are pretty much the same in all villages. Concepts of karma, dharma, and jati find concrete expression everywhere, and there are consistent regularities in patterns for the production, distribution, and consumption of goods.

When individual communities are closely examined, the general consistencies imposed by shared tradition and technology tend to recede into the background, and sharp differences begin to appear. Gopalpur, Namhalli, and Elephant all have concepts of karma and dharma, but the meaning and impact of these concepts is different in each of the villages. Everywhere in South India men yoke oxen to their plows, but on closer examination the men, the oxen, and the plows prove to be subtly different. Each village is constructed from the same basic plan, but in some villages part of the plan was lost and shortages of materials resulted in last-minute alterations.

Neither the plan nor the environment causes a particular sort of village to develop. Rather, the form of the village and of its ecological system depends upon complex interactions between plans and realities. Within the ecological system, many simple causal relationships obtain. If there is abundant water and level ground, it is likely that irrigation works will be built and rice agriculture undertaken. If there is black soil suitable for white sorghum, it is a safe bet that white sorghum will be grown on it. Such simple relationships explain much about any single village, but a broader understanding requires a more detailed knowledge of interactions among the kinds of people that founded the village and the specific combination of environmental circumstances that they encountered.

Elephant, for example, developed around a religious institution, a mathe, which seems to have been constructed to provide a resting place for pilgrims traversing the hilly and forested country near the banks of the sacred Cauvery River. In consequence, the original settlers were members of a priestly jati belonging to the Lingayat sect. Being vegetarians, they never undertook the raising of sheep and goats, and they appear to have resisted the migration of irreligious (meat-eating) persons into the village. Elephant's religious bias, combined with its isolation in what is now a protected forest, limited its growth and prevented it from developing into a "normal," multijati village.

In the Gopalpur region, where most villages contain a variety of jatis, the particular assortment of jatis to be found in a given community seems to have been dictated in many cases by the status and occupation of individual jatis. For the most part, the better lands and the wealthier villages appear to be dominated by members of relatively high-ranking yeoman farmer jatis, while the poorer lands and villages tend to contain lower-ranking and less wealthy jatis. The clearest illustration of this process is to be found in the relatively recent movement of the Lambadi jati into the Gopalpur region. Traditionally, the Lambadi were a migratory jati whose karma involved the transportation of goods from place to place on the backs of bullocks. As roads and railroads were constructed, the Lambadi were afflicted by poverty, classified as a "criminal" jati, and eventually settled on sandy and infertile lands. Possessing a cultural tradition and language which evidently originated in northwestern India, the Lambadi hamlets differ markedly from other communities.

Within the Gopalpur region, concentrations of Shepherds are found where there are abundant marginal lands suitable for sheep grazing. Saltmakers are found near sources of briny water; Flower Gardeners, where irrigation water is available; Stoneworkers, near outcrops of granite. By contrast, Barbers and Washermen, whose occupations depend on population density, are distributed everywhere in numbers roughly proportionate to village size. Because different jatis follow different social and religious practices and place a heavier emphasis on some aspects of the South Indian world view than on others, it follows that the ecological relationships of any particular village will be greatly affected by the special kinds of people who come to constitute its membership. The environment influences the selection of jatis that will ultimately form a community, and the kinds of jatis forming the community influence the kinds of relationships that will be formed between the community and its environment.

In addition to these Founder and Member effects, the nature of any community is deeply influenced by the restrictions that determine the location of its lands and its village site. The accompanying map (Figure 4) of the villages that surround Gopalpur illustrates

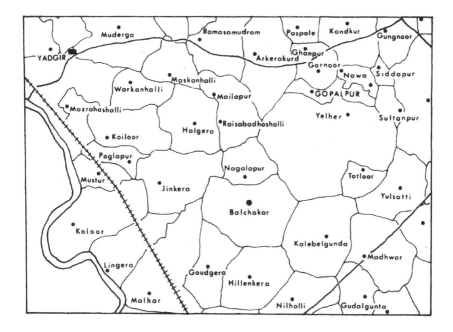

Figure 4

the variation in size of the landholdings of different villages as well as the seemingly unpatterned nature of village boundaries and site locations. The lack of pattern is a reflection not of irrationality but of the need to take many considerations into account in establishing boundaries and locations.

New village boundaries must be established with due regard to the existing boundaries of other villages. Over a period of time, negotiations and conflict result in further modifications of the boundaries until they are stabilized. The map reflects village boundaries at one point in time, and since it was drawn the village of Ganpur (Gannapur) has moved to the site of a defunct village labeled Gornoor on the map. Gopalpur has expanded its lands to the east and south at the expense of Arkera Khurd and Yelher. Such readjustments reflect factors of convenience and efficiency in caring for agricultural lands. When a farmer owns a field that is distant from his own village and close to another, his crops are likely to be stolen. He also faces obvious problems in transporting manure to the distant field and in maintaining the constant supervision required for the care of growing crops. Thus, he must either sell his field or move to the other village.

In general, village boundaries must be located to permit the transportation of bullocks, plows, manure, and labor to the fields without too much loss of time and energy. Here the principal limiting factor is often the need to carry adequate quantities of manure to unirrigated fields. Manure moved by headload, as in Elephant, cannot easily be carried for more than a mile or two. The limit on transportation by cartload seems to be about four miles on good terrain. In practice, considering the fact that most fields are not on roads and must be reached by roundabout routes, the ideal radius of village boundaries is probably closer to two miles than four.

Rice crops require extensive care and supervision. The paddies are muddy swamps for at least four months out of the year. For these reasons, and because rice paddies are extremely productive, villages specializing in rice agriculture tend to be within shouting distance of each other. Villages with a mixture of irrigated and unirrigated lands are likely to have their access to distant millet fields restricted by a barrier of muddy rice paddies.

Although terrain features sometimes encourage village specialization in a single crop, the usual pattern is one of sloping lands that offer different soil types and conditions suitable for a variety of crops. Because different crops are planted and harvested at different times, the farmer who owns several plots of different types of land has an economic advantage in that he and his family can keep busy for eight or nine months out of the year instead of only four or five. Where possible, a village boundary will be drawn so as to provide a mixture of rice lands, garden lands, and dry lands. Boundaries also tend to be drawn along the tops of mountain ridges or down the center of impassable streams. Wastelands, useful for grazing or the collection of firewood but unsuitable for agriculture, are found within the boundaries of most villages.

Still another influence on community village boundaries is the location of the village site. A settlement should not ordinarily be constructed on valuable agricultural land; it should be reasonably close to sources of drinking water; and it should have sufficient exposure to the wind to reduce the threat of mosquitoes and other insects and to keep the houses cool.

Village site and boundary locations based on human decisions are critical determinants of the kind of natural environment a village will have. Because these Locational effects, like Founder effects, are logically prior to other aspects of village life, they can be regarded as causal factors that play a role in determining subsequent ecological relationships. When Founder and Locational effects are treated as causes, it is important to remember that they are not fully independent. They are a result of complex interactions between the larger environment and the regional culture and society.

The importance of the village site and boundary derives from the fact that most people in South India live in tightly packed clusters of houses usually labeled "nucleated villages." A number of factors contribute to the desirability of this settlement pattern. Scattered farmhouses may lack access to sources of drinking water. The lands belonging to an individual farmer are often widely scattered as a result of inheritance patterns and the economic advantages of owning a variety of types of land. Harvested grain and cattle are portable forms of wealth that cannot be guarded effectively by the limited personnel available in an isolated farmhouse. Unsettled political conditions, drought, and crop failure led in traditional times to the development of patterns of cattle raiding, banditry, and warfare, against which single households could provide no effective defense. In addition, traditional governments probably encouraged the development of nucleated villages in order to control the population or to combat banditry and cattle raiding.

Where scattered farmsteads do occur in South India, they generally appear in regions where intensive gardening is practiced, where the terrain is rugged, and where centralized political organizations were historically unstable. In Namhalli, garden crops must be constantly protected from thieves and monkeys, and the family member responsible for the garden often takes up residence within it. Where gardening is the principal means of subsistence, the temptation to establish the entire household in the garden appears to be irresistible.

Within the village boundaries, agricultural resources—such as types of soil, patterns of rainfall, and potentialities for irrigation and well construction—influence the selection of particular crops and crop types. This selection is also influenced by market conditions and by the availability of capital and manpower within the community. When portions of the village lands have been set aside as forest, pasture, and dry or irrigated lands, and when particular crops have been selected, irreversible changes are likely to take place in the environment. To a degree, then, early decisions about land use involve long-term commitments to particular agricultural practices and ecological relationships.

Such commitments have far-reaching consequences for future relationships between communities and for the kinds of technology and social organization that will be maintained within each. Rice lands, for example, usually require a heavy initial investment in the preparation of land, a heavy commitment of labor for the care and harvesting of the crop, and, because yields are likely to be high, the development of appropriate mechanisms for selling or otherwise distributing the harvested grain.

For all crops and crop types, the principal source of capital and labor is a farm manager who is usually either a small landowner or a sharecropper. Members of this yeoman class provide year-round maintenance of the land and make decisions about the crops to be planted and the times at which the various operations are to be carried out. The acreage of land that may be efficiently operated by an individual farmer is determined by the nature of the crop. Granted a certain amount of variation, the selection of particular crop types in a given community determines a "farmer/land" ratio that establishes within relatively narrow limits the number of farmers that can be effectively maintained. Although a large household may contain several adult male farmers, the discrepancy between the number of farmers and the number of farm households is usually small.

For unirrigated lands dedicated to millet crops like ragi, the appropriate ratio is generally considered to be five or six acres per farmer. A village with 300 acres of land in ragi would support somewhere between 50 and 60 farmers. Rice and garden agriculture, by contrast, may involve a farmer/land ratio of less than one acre per farmer. Because each village has its own unique distribution of lands and crops, each tends to have a unique ratio. Where a farmer owns dry and irrigated lands that require care during different seasons, he may be able to manage maximum-sized fields of both types; where several kinds of land require care during the same season, the total number of acres he can handle is correspondingly diminished.

Because grain crops require animals for manure and traction, the number and kinds of animals in the village, as well as the number of farmers, is influenced by the nature of the crops grown. Just as the selection of crop types influences the population of farmers and animals, so a shortage of manure, animal traction, or manpower influences crop yields. Plant, animal, and human populations are systematically linked so that changes in the numbers or kinds of any one will produce changes in the others. With the exception of villages dedicated to gardening or to highly specialized production, the basic ecological relationship in South Indian agriculture is the correlation among crops, animals, and human beings, each biological population being dependent on the others.

In addition to yeoman farmers, three other broad classes of people are likely to be found in South Indian communities: investors, specialists, and laborers. Where crop yields and consequently land values are high, ownership of the land and the crops is likely to be held by investors. These may be moneylenders, landlords, government officials, or religious institutions, and usually they do not undertake the direct management of land. Generally they furnish credit and sometimes they provide protection or organizational assistance to the farmer in return for a sometimes substantial portion of the crop. Traditionally, and particularly on land made valuable by the construction of major irrigation works requiring large capital investment, the farmer remained a tenant or sharecropper while ownership was retained by the government or wealthy landlords. Lands that are highly productive, regardless of the expense required to make them productive, are likely to be owned by investors.

Because agriculture is a risky business, farmers prefer to use borrowed capital to meet expenditures for seed, equipment, and labor. If the farmer owns valuable land, he is likely to mortgage it. In many cases, his indebtedness to a wealthy patron is an essential means of providing himself and his family with social and political support. If a village can suport a class of investors, it will, and the amount of yield per farmer is the principal determinant of the number of investors that can be supported.

The selection of crops ordinarily grown within the community establishes seasonal needs for labor beyond those that can be supplied by a farmer and his family. A farmer and his bullocks can plow a six-acre millet field, but a force of between 10 and 20 laborers is required for weeding and harvesting. If yields are small and there is a single major planting season, the excess labor must be imported because the village cannot support a resident labor force. Since the villages near Elephant are located at different altitudes, farmers are able to serve as laborers in neighboring villages during the seasons when there is no work in their own. In Elephant, crop yields are small, and little grain is available for sale. Lacking cash, the village tends to solve its labor problems through exchanges between villages, often involving relatives. This pattern of labor exchange among yeoman farmers inhibits the development of a laborer class.

Where rice and garden crops produce high yields and a continuing demand for labor, a sizable class of landless laborers is likely to develop. If a farmer requires a laborer's services for six to nine months out of the year, he is likely to give the laborer subsistence and a small annual payment in return for a year's work. A laborer who must work for several different farmers to obtain his subsistence is likely to be paid by the day in grain or cash. The particular selection of crops within a village thus influences the source and number of landless laborers resident within it.

Every village requires the services of specialists who repair farm equipment, manufacture household utensils, or provide personal services. The size of the specialist class within a village depends on the number of people resident there, the size of crop yields, and the extent to which those yields are retained by farmers and laborers. If an investor class, inevitably small in numbers, absorbs a substantial proportion of the yield, farmers and laborers will be unable to afford the services of many specialists, and their number will be correspondingly reduced. If a village consists almost entirely of small farmers who raise barely enough to support themselves, the farmers will lack the means to support a large class of specialists and the village will be small.

The selection of crop types thus exerts a powerful influence on the relative number of investors, farmers, laborers, and specialists residing in a village. The distribution of these classes of persons has a great deal to do with the kinds of jatis that are present. A village consisting almost entirely of farmers, like Elephant, is likely to derive most of its population form one or two farmer jatis of approximately equal rank. A wealthy village containing an investor jati such as the Brahmans and large numbers of laborers will tend to be divided between high-ranking and low-ranking jatis. Because members of the specialist class are in separate jatis practicing such specialities as blacksmithing, haircutting, potmaking, carpentry, and priestcraft, villages that contain large numbers of specialists automatically contain a variety of jatis.

The world view of hierarchically arranged jatis, combined with local patterns establishing the rank of the various jatis, influences the character of social relationships within each community. A village of farmers and specialists of approximately equal rank is more egalitarian than is a village that consists primarily of investors and their landless servants.

Within a given region, and here the Gopalpur region serves as the principle example, differences in the environments of different communities lead to the development of strong contrasts among them. While some villages in the Gopalpur region are hard to classify, on the whole four well-defined types can be established in terms of population size and related characteristics: hamlets, small villages, medium villages, and large villages.

A hamlet is a minuscule community with between 15 and 80 households of which all but a few belong to the same—usually low-ranking—jati. It has no members of service jatis—no Barber, no Priest, no Blacksmith. There are no stores or shops, no large houses, no major religious establishments, no schools, no post offices, and no resident government officials. Hamlets are rarely close to roads or bus lines. They often have difficulty obtaining drinking water. Religious rituals and other organized events rarely take place in them. Government officials never visit them, and government maps and documents do not recognize their existence. On the other hand, thefts, quarrels, fights, and party conflicts rarely occur in hamlets.

Economically, hamlets tend to be dependent on a single, relatively unproductive crop, usually one of the millets. Cultivation of such a crop is possible during less than six months out of the year, and yields are generally too small to support the farmer and his family throughout the year. Hence it is necessary for the residents of hamlets to supplement their income through banditry or migratory labor. The extreme poverty of most hamlets makes it impossible for them to support any resident class of farm laborers.

Very often hamlets are totally dependent on wealthy men in neighboring villages who rule with an iron hand by granting and withholding loans and jobs. Hamlets not dominated by such moneylenders are subject to domination by minor government officials, who may refuse to grant permanent landownership to residents and then may exact lavish "gifts" to compensate them for permitting "illegal" occupation of the land.

Although located outside the Gopalpur region, Elephant approximates the model of a hamlet given above. The chief difference between Elephant and more typical hamlets is that Elephant is somewhat larger than most, large enough, in fact, to support a religious establishment and to carry out an annual round of religious ceremonies and dramas. With increasing population and the development of a dairy industry, Elephant has more and more closely approached the small village type, even though religious restrictions have limited the movement of additional jatis into the community.

In the Gopalpur region, hamlets are often located at considerable distances from other settlements. Where hamletlike settlements take the form of "streets"—ghettos or colonies existing as part of or in close connection with a larger village—they appear to be different in form and are perhaps best regarded as representing individual jatis within a larger multijati community.

Small villages contain between 90 and 140 households. Their ecological situation differs from that of hamlets in that they generally contain some patches of good or irrigated soil, even though the bulk of their soil may be no better than that of the average hamlet. Although the small village may have much the same farmer/land ratio as the hamlet, it has more land and more farmers. By shifting their agricultural operations from one crop to another, farmers in small villages may be employed for nine or ten months out of the year and thus are able to produce a yield sufficient to support their families throughout the year and to pay for a substantial range of specialized services.

Because the population of a small village is sufficient to support a number of full-time specialists, such villages usually contain representatives of a variety of jatis. Although a single Farmer jati may comprise about half the population, other Farmer jatis may be present in significant numbers. Small villages are frequently divided into hostile "parties," often formed around opposed lineages within a single numerically dominant jati. People living in small villages report a high incidence of thefts, quarrels, fights, and party conflicts.

Small villages also tend to have a high incidence of such co-operative efforts as village dramas, hymn-singing groups, wrestling teams, and religious ceremonies. The small villages divided into hostile parties are the ones that undertake large festivals designed to attract visitors from neighboring villages. Such villages are too large to control conflict easily through informal "face-to-face" mechanisms and too small to control conflict through the introduction of formal police mechanisms. Periodic large festivals and other cooperative efforts may compel periodic reductions in the intensity of conflicts and may serve to demonstrate community harmony to outsiders.

Although small villages are sometimes dominated by a single wealthy Headman and moneylender, they do not generally produce a crop surplus sufficient to support a sizable investor class. Most such villages do, however, support small numbers of landless laborers. The most common pattern of income distribution reflects the numerical and economic predominance of the yeoman farmer, and the predominant pattern of interpersonal relationships is one of equality, democracy, and conflict.

Although most small villages contain one or two tobacco and spice shops, they never contain cloth stores or larger shops. And although they generally contain specialists providing a substantial number of necessary services, they are always dependent on neighboring larger villages for some services.

Medium-sized villages contain between 150 and 290 households and have substantial acreages of irrigated paddy lands or other especially productive agricultural resources. Their farmer population and agricultural yields are sufficient to permit the permanent residence of a full range of specialized jatis and occupational groups. The medium-sized village receives relatively few goods and services from nearby villages. Its population and tax base is sufficient to support a range of government services unavailable to small villages. All medium-sized villages possess primary schools, and many possess middle schools, roughly equivalent to American junior high schools. These villages are regularly visited by policemen, village improvement workers, and other government officials. Most medium-sized villages contain representatives of more than one important Farmer jati. Conflict within these villages tends to occur between jatis of approximately equal rank. Like the conflict that occurs in small villages, this is referred to locally as "party" conflict and tends to take the form of periodic outbreaks. There is some evidence that on the whole medium-sized villages have less conflict than small villages. Although this can be attributed in part to structural factors that make it difficult to divide the population into two roughly equal parties, the more or less continuous presence of policemen, relatively well-educated middle-school teachers, and other government officials may inhibit the escalation of conflict. Some medium-sized villages, like some small villages, are dominated by the head of a single powerful landed family. Domination of this kind may also serve to suppress conflict, at least during the lifetime of the family head.

Large villages contain 300 or more households and have large acreages of rich agricultural lands, most often rice land producing several crops each year. Such villages usually contain weekly markets; large, permanent cloth shops; middle schools; and other facilities including medical dispensaries, police substations, and community development centers. Usually, they include several hamlets within their official boundaries and provides a variety of services to nearby small villages.

Large villages tend to contain several families with sufficient wealth to give them region-wide political and economic importance. Such families often own jeeps or tractors and generally have enough money and power to give them substantial control of local government. As befits a rural aristocracy, these families stand at the apex of patronage pyramids (they are the moneylenders' moneylenders) and play an essential role in providing credit in their own and neighboring villages. Most such families possess retainers, often recruited from the impoverished populations of nearby hamlets, who are prepared to enforce their patrons' will by beating up uncooperative clients or robbing the houses of competing patrons.

Party conflict in large villages is endemic and seems to arise out of the struggles for power of rival "Big men." These villages seem to contain relatively few specialists and yeoman farmers. Much of the population is too poor to utilize specialists or too rich to rely on local services. Conflict between the very rich and the very poor is obscured in most smaller villages by the fact that most people are farmers or specialists. In a few large villages, conflict between competing patrons alternates with conflict between the patrons and the resident landless laborers.

In directing attention to the subtle and complicated relationships that develop between villages and the agricultural lands surrounding them, I have tried to present agricultural ecology as an outcome of intersecting forces represented by the traditional world view and technology on the one hand and by the village lands on the other. Village boundaries are fixed as a result of decision-making processes in which traditional values are weighed against the demands of efficient agricultural production. Once the boundaries are established, decisions on crop plantings are made by gauging which crops will grow best and which will fetch the best prices in the regional market. The selection of particular crops or crop types in turn affects the number of persons and animals the village can support. It also affects the kinds of jatis and social classes that will be present and the kinds of groupings and task forces that will be needed if the crops are to be grown efficiently. Population size, as well as other factors considered above, plays an important role in determining the type of community likely to be established. The status of the community as a hamlet, small village, medium village, or large village has sweeping effects on every aspect of social organization, from the existence of conflict to the distribution of wealth and power.

At every point, the systematic relationships between the rural community and the lands within its boundaries are modified and directed by other kinds of relationships. The rural community must not only produce crops but must also develop and maintain the human population that produces the crops. Part of the overall environment of any community is the human environment. The next chapter considers the human environment of the South Indian village and the manner in which ecological relationships involve the special properties of the human species.

Gopalpur 1960.
Man carrying water
from the stream. A
woman would carry
one pot on her head
and another resting on
her hip.

Namhalli 1952. Levelling a rice paddy.

Namhalli 1952.
Boys playing in the
river on a raft made of
banana stalks. Rice and
garden lands are in the
background. Both boys
have now completed
high school and are
working in factories.

Namhalli 1952. Watering bullocks at the irrigation canal.
Gardens are in the background.

Namhalli 1960. A schoolboy irrigating the garden.

Gopalpur 1966. Transporting jolla hay to the village for cattle fodder.

Namhalli 1960. Threshing ragi with a stone roller.

Gopalpur 1966. Winnowing jolla. Waiting for the wind to blow.

Carrying manure to the millet fields.

Loading a crop of beans into a blanket before transporting them to the village.

Elephant 1952.
When the wells dry up,
drinking water must be
carried from the valley
floor.

Namhalli 1962.
A drinking water well constructed by the government. Such wells are unlikely to harbor cholera or other disease organisms.

Gopalpur 1960.
Washing clothes in the
stream. Drinking water is
obtained from shallow
holes scooped in the sand.

**Elephant 1952.
Threshing millet
with flails.**

Gopalpur 1960. Washing dishes in the street outside the house.

Namhalli 1952. Blacksmith working at forge. The blacksmith is now a factory worker.

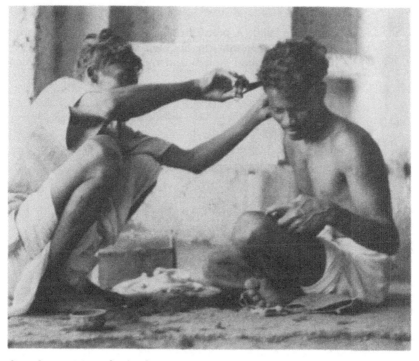

Gopalpur 1960. The barber provides a weekly shave and haircut to his clients in exchange for an annual payment in grain. .

Gopalpur 1960. A potter brings wares from a neighboring village for cash sale. In his own village, he functions as part of the jajmani system and receives an annual payment.

Gopalpur 1960. Splashing drinking water into a pot. Cholera epidemics resulting from water pollution occur every few years.

Gopalpur 1960. At Gopalpur's annual festival each jati constructs a line of fireplaces on which to prepare meat from sheep sacrificed in honor of Gopalpur's Muslim saint.

Gopalpur 1966. A Lingagyat priest conducts a private school at Gopalpur.

Gopalpur 1960.
Bullocks and children
share the village street.

Elephant 1966. The village children pose for a photograph in
the street. The population explosion began with the introduction
of a busline and the sale of milk to Bangalore City.

Elephant 1952. People watching the ceremony at the shrine of
Mariamma.

Namhalli 1952. Celebration of a wedding.

Namhalli 1960. After their baths, Lingayat women mark their foreheads with sacred cow dung ash. Printed blouses and saris trailing on the ground reflect an urban style of dress.

Chapter 5

POPULATION REGULATION

When our attention is focused on agricultural production, it is easy to interpret much that happens within the community as adjustment and adaptation to the needs of domesticated plants and animals. And without question the efficient cultivation of any crop requires that highly specific services be provided to the crop at particular times and in particular ways. In ecological terms, the priority of domesticated plants is indisputable—everything depends on the capture of solar energy through photosynthesis. On the other hand, plants, animals, and people exist in a tight symbiotic relationship, such that the survival of each is dependent on the survival of the others. In the total ecological system, the requirements for the production, care, and feeding of the human crop are just as important as the requirements for the production of plants and animals. This chapter considers the problem of maintaining adequate numbers and varieties of human beings within the community.

In traditional South India, epidemic disease, crop failure, and war resulted in a relatively high mortality. Although these catastrophic events periodically decimated the population of many parts of South India, endemic diseases affecting children—malaria, worms, intestinal ailments—were the major cause of human death. Consequently, the traditional community consisted of a relatively small number of adults and a relatively large number of children destined never to become adults. The accompanying summary of census materials collected in Elephant in 1952 demonstrates this type of population pattern. There are 65 children less than five years old and 32 children whose ages range from five to less than ten. The village contains 36 women of childbearing age, not all of whom are fertile. The fertile women must be almost constantly pregnant to compensate for the high rate of child mortality. The children who survive must be given the best care possible, or they too will become part of the infant mortality statistics. The total manpower requirement of a village is not determined solely by agricultural problems, and the need for female field labor must always be balanced against the need to mother small children.

The capacity of a village to provide the manpower required for its various tasks and duties also involves the maintenance of an appropriate distribution of types and varieties of people—old and young, male and female, with a variety of skills and resources. To the extent that any disproportion in numbers is due to chance or other uncontrolled forces, it can be a significant adaptive problem.

In 1952, Elephant had 70 females and 82 males fifteen years of age and over. The consequences for agricultural production are likely to be a lack of correspondence between manpower requirements and the manpower actually present. Such a lack of correspondence can only be remedied by population exchanges between villages, a matter to be discussed later.

The problem of maintaining an equilibrium between manpower requirements and population size is accentuated by periodic catastrophes. The Mysore War (between Citizen Tipu Sultan and the British), which ended in 1800, is estimated to have reduced the population of Mysore by 50 percent. The famine of 1877, which affected most of South India, and the influenza epidemic of 1919 also produced sharp reductions in population. The small number of persons in Elephant who were 30 years of age or over in 1952 can be attributed to the influenza epidemic.

Although there has been an upward trend in Namhalli's population, which can be attributed to modernization and increased agricultural production, the general pattern of population fluctuation in South India suggests an alternation between population shortage and surplus. A relatively slow increase followed by rapid decimation in war, epidemic, or famine has profound implications for village social structure. During periods of population increase the chances of forming extended family households are increased, because there is a greater likelihood that married couples will pro-

duce several sons who will then remain in the household. A pattern
of alternating population growth and decline would explain the
emphasis in the traditional world view on having many children
in large households. The possibilties for preferred marriages to
close relatives are also increased when each mother has large numbers of living children, because there are more likely to be suitable
partners of appropriate age and sex.

Table 2. Elephant Population
by Age Groups, 1952

Age	Male	Female
95–99	0	1
90–94	1	0
85–89	0	0
80–84	1	0
75–59	0	0
70–74	0	1
65–69	1	1
60–64	1	0
55–59	5	0
50–54	6	4
45–49	3	3
40–44	8	5
35–39	7	4
30–34	7	11
25–29	11	7
20–24	19	14
15–19	12	19
10–14	15	17
5– 9	19	13
0– 4	33	32

In terms of agricultural production, a pattern of periodic population losses would regularly remove marginal lands from cultivation and concentrate agricultural effort on lands near the village
that can be adequately manured. Such automatic fallowing of marginal lands might have been necessary to maintain their fertility.
During the cyclical population increases when marginal lands were
again cultivated, there may have been a corresponding decline in
the animal population (with less grazing land) and consequently
in nutrition. An increasingly dense and malnourished population

combined with the increasing use of marginal lands would set the stage for emigration or for territorial aggrandizement leading to warfare. Crop failure and epidemic disease would also result from the overutilization of land, malnutrition, and rising population density. The years immediately following a severe population decline would be golden years characterized by large families, abundant food, comparative freedom from illness, and a comparative absence of cattle raiding, crop theft, and warfare.

Variations in village population, while they may sometimes be dramatic, are probably not as great as variations in the size and sex and age distributions of such constituent units as households, neighborhoods, lineages, and jatis. Table 3 shows the distribution of family types among the households in Elephant in 1952. Out of 58 households of permanent residents, there were 8 extended family households, consisting of sets of at least two brothers and their wives, and 37 nuclear family households, consisting of husband and wife, their children if any, and sometimes the husband's mother. Although the extended family household is the ideal, it can only be formed when a family contains two or more male children who survive to become adults. In a stable population in which the average family produces two surviving children, a household containing two brothers is likely to occur only 25 percent of the time. Without extensive merging of nuclear families through adoption or other means, the extended family household must always occur less frequently than the nuclear family household. Because an extended family must comprise at least two nuclear families, it follows that the eight extended families in Elephant comprise no fewer than sixteen nuclear families, a sizable proportion of the total probably approaching the maximum number of extended families that could be formed.

Out of the 58 households in Elephant, 13 were in some way broken or unusual. It is not always possible to form and maintain a nuclear family, let alone an extended one. As noted in earlier chapters, the household plays a key role in agricultural production. Among nuclear families, it is helpful if the children are old enough to assist their parents with such chores as herding cattle, bringing water, or guarding fields, or if there is a grandparent to care for young children. If an efficient family work team consists of father, mother, son, and daughter, only 26 out of the 58 families meet this criterion. Out of the 26 that contain both sons and daughters, only

Table 3. Family Types in Elephant, 1952

	Children				
	Childless	Both Sexes	Male Only	Female Only	Total
NUCLEAR (37)					
Husband and Wife	3	19	4	3	29
(one husband uxorilocal)					
Husband, wife, and husband's mother	2	3	0	3	8
FRATERNAL EXTENDED (8)					
Two brothers and wives and one or two parents of brothers	2	3	1	1	7
(one household of four brothers included)					
Two brothers without parents	0	1	0	0	1
UNCLASSIFIED (13)					
Wife, no husband	0	1	1	2	4
Father, daughter, daughter's daughter, son					1
Mother, son, two son's sons, one son's daughter					1
Father, three sons					1
Mother, daughter, daughter's son					1
Husband, two wives, son					1
Husband, family not yet migrated					1
Woman alone					1
Woman alone					1
Husband, wife, adopted daughter					1
TRANSIENT AND OF DIFFERENT JATI (6)					
Husband, wife, two daughters, mother (Madiga)					1
Male teacher unmarried (Gauda Lingayat)					1
Mother, three sons (Lingayat Washerman)					1
Mother, son, son's daughter (Lingayat Washerman)					1
Husband, wife, two sons, one daughter (Basket Weaver)					1
Husband, wife, daughter (Basket Weaver)					1

a few have children old enough to contribute importantly to the work of the household.

Census information from Elephant indicates that the individual household is not a standardized economic unit capable of performing the full range of agricultural and other operations. Except for very short time periods, it is impossible for a household to have the exact number of males and females of appropriate age for the efficient performance of all its required tasks. But the household composition of any South Indian village is only partly the result of statistical variation and accident. A variety of techniques are consistently applied that have the effect of replacing absent family members and "transferring" surplus population.

In an environment subject to numerous endemic and epidemic diseases and in which famine, malnutrition, and chronic ill-health are all too common, the production of at least one male adult per household—a mandate of the South Indian world view—is no easy matter. Religious ceremonies connected with betrothal marriage, puberty, and nuptial marriage contain elaborate symbolism dedicated to the promotion of the bride's fertility. Following nuptial marriage, when the bride begins to cohabit with her husband, the first signs of pregnancy are eagerly awaited, especially if the bride is married to an older brother. At the first sign, the bride is frequently sent to the house of her parents where she is treated with almost complete indulgence. It is an obligation, often fulfilled, to give pregnant women any kind of food they ask for:

Pregnant women always like to eat whatever they see. If they aren't allowed to eat what they see, they won't be happy. Once I went to a fair to purchase a pair of bullocks. On the way I saw a pregnant woman, very beautiful. At that moment another man was passing with a ripe jackfruit. The woman was telling her husband that she wanted some jackfruit. The jackfruit man cut the fruit and gave her half and went away. [Namhalli, 1952]

Pregnant women are given a kind of red earth to eat as a means of preventing anemia. Nonvegetarian and even vegetarian women, to whom alcoholic beverages are technically forbidden, often drink palm wine—rich in yeast—during their pregnancies. Especially after the seventh month, women are not permitted to leave their houses during eclipses of the sun or moon. People in Namhalli know of one man in a neighboring village who was born with deformed legs after his mother was caught in an eclipse.

The sex of the child can be determined by the activity of the mother. If she is talkative and active, a male child is expected. More certain knowledge can be obtained from a specialist:

B can determine the sex of a child before delivery. A few days ago, C came to get castor oil and a *mantram* [incantation] before the delivery. B repeats the mantram over the castor oil and stirs it with a small stick.

If the oil becomes watery, then a female child will be born; if it becomes sticky, a male will be born. If the oil becomes very sticky, like honey, B will say that the child died in the womb. [Namhalli, 1952]

When delivery is expected, a special ceremony is held for the benefit of the pregnant woman, and she receives an oil bath, new clothing, and gifts of jewelry. Special food is prepared, and neighbors are invited to join the feast. The husband and wife sit on a special platform facing north or east. Family elders pass sacred fire (*arathi*) and colored water in front of the couple's faces. After the ceremony has been completed, the wife is taken to her parents' house, and the husband does not shave or cut his hair until the day of delivery:

My father asked me to go to my wife's place on the day of delivery. My parents believed that after I showed my face, the delivery would be safe. Nowadays, parents need not order their sons to go out and see their wives' faces. They go of their own accord. If the husband doesn't come, the wife may not have breast milk, and there are other bad effects. If she sees her husband, she is happy and the pains of delivery are reduced. [Namhalli, 1952]

At her parents' house, the pregnant woman is served special foods, particularly sweets. She receives frequent hot water baths and wears good clothing and jewelry. She is asked not to work, not to be jealous, not to be filled with hate, and not to be angry: "If she acts that way, the newborn child will have the same character." In many families the pregnant woman is asked to worship the goddess Gowri daily.

Despite the indulgence of pregnant women, miscarriages and stillbirths are frequent. In Namhalli, interviews with women over the age of 40 indicated that 11 out of 29 had produced no living children. Among those that had borne living children, the average number of births reported was 8.11, of whom 4.45 were living.

When repeated pregnancies fail to produce live births, or when conception fails to occur, various remedies are attempted. In Namhalli, a couple may first try to improve their fertility by worshiping the "snake stones" (*nagara kallu*) located on a special platform where a neem tree and a pipal tree have been planted. If this fails, pilgrimages to distant shrines may be attempted. Frequently it is assumed by both the married couple and the village gossips, especially the latter, that infertility is the result of sins committed by the husband or wife in this life or a previous one. According to one folktale, for example, a man who had no children once went to his guru (religious teacher) for advice. The guru informed him that he would have children but told him to bury each child in the village cemetery as it was born. The man, as would any loyal devotee, did as he was told. When the man had buried eight children, he complained to the guru and was told to go to the cemetery at night and listen. He heard the eight children talking, and the first seven all said they were people from whom the man had borrowed money without returning it. They had been reborn as his children so they could torment him for the remainder of his life. Later, the man rescued the innocent eighth child and lived happily ever after.

The efforts a young couple expend in arranging for the conception of their first child depend very much on their attachment to each other and on which of the spouses is considered to be infertile. Very often, if a wife fails to conceive within a reasonable length of time, she is simply expelled from the household and sent back to her parents. Less frequently—particularly in recent years, since polygyny has been outlawed—the bride's sister or some other suitable female is selected as a second wife.

Where a strong attachment exists between husband and wife, or where the husband appears to be infertile, an attempt is often made to adopt a younger child of a close relative. Gopalpur genealogies reaching back to the nineteenth century provide a few cases of outright purchase of a child from strangers for adoption.

For purposes of family inheritance and for a variety of religious reasons, it is imperative that every married couple produce at least one son. Inevitably there is sharp disappointment if the firstborn child is a girl. When my own firstborn turned out to be a girl, the universal response in Gopalpur was, "Don't feel too badly about it; after all, she can take care of your son when he is born." In fact, most living and remembered firstborn children are males. For example, the 1952 census of Elephant lists 29 families in which the first of two or more children is male and 10 families in which the first child is female. In 20 families the last child is male, and in 19, female. The most reasonable explanation for the mysterious shortage of firstborn female children is disappointment resulting in neglect of both mother and daughter. In Namhalli, female children and late-born male children are rarely reported as having ever received medical treatment.

Another explanation of unbalanced sex ratios may involve differences in patterns of resort to the postpartum sex taboo, in which wives and husbands are kept apart after the birth of a child. An old man from Namhalli raised in a large and traditional extended family explains:

> In those years the spacing between children was not less than four years. The elderly women in the house and the wife did not allow the male members to visit their wives for two years after the birth of a child with the intention of having the child grow strong by taking its mother's milk. By the end of four years both husband and wife would feel as if they had just been married. Many times my wife sent me out. My wife and I did not talk before my parents. Nowadays, by the eleventh month of the child, there will be a second child in the womb. How can you expect them to have good bones and be strong? [1952]

Following the birth of a child, both child and mother remain in a state of ritual impurity. In Elephant, despite daily hot water baths, this state of contamination continues until the seventh day after birth. On this day, the village priest (*svamiji*) conducts a cleansing ceremony and gives the child a name of his choosing. On the eleventh day after birth, the mother is dressed in new clothing and jewelry. Close relatives and friends are invited to a meal, and the child is placed in a cradle decorated with flowers. Five elderly women who have not been widowed, divorced, or remarried then give names to the child. The first name is usually that of the child's lineage god, and the second is usually the one the parents wish the child to have, often that of the father's father.

Namhalli's midwife gives the following account of her career and practices.

> Since 1920, I have been the only midwife in this village. Before that, my mother was the midwife. She trained me in that sacred work, and I am doing it according to her instructions. I have attended almost all the births in this village since 1920. So far, I have had no failures; that is, none of the women I have attended died. There were two cases in which I could not help as the babies were turned crosswise in the womb. When I understood that those cases were beyond my knowledge, I asked the husbands to take their wives to the hospital. I accompanied them.
>
> Whenever I get a call from a house for my services, I go there and

ask the pregnant woman about her bowels and find out how frequently she is having pains. I give her a half spoonful of *hacce bija* [a kind of medicinal seed] in a cup of cold water. Within half an hour, the delivery will be completed, as those seeds are very effective in increasing the frequency of the labor pains. I put a lot of castor oil on my hands before going to work. Right after delivery, I give the woman the weight of one bean seed of asafetida in a ragi ball. This prevents her from getting any cold or fever. If the delivery has been slow, I warm a handful of tender tamarind leaves in a thin cloth and heat the hollow of the stomach. This relieves the aftereffects and the pain. After delivery, if the placenta does not come out in time, I place a long hair inside the woman's throat. This makes her cough heavily, and the placenta soon comes out. A small amount of musk or two teaspoonfuls of brandy administered every day for five days will also help to prevent cold and fever, but these are more expensive than asafetida. [1952]

After delivery, the Namhalli midwife cuts the umbilical cord, then washes the baby with warm water and places it in a winnowing tray that has been covered with straw and clean cloth. A thin piece of cloth or mosquito netting is placed over the baby. To prevent illness the baby is usually branded on the stomach with a red-hot iron. Depending on jati membership, the mother is denied certain foods for several days after the delivery. The child receives no food for the first two or three days after birth except for a little donkey's milk or warm castor oil intended to clean out its stomach. On the third or fourth day, the child begins to nurse. It receives its first solid food, usually boiled rice, when it is six months old.

When the child is about seven months old, a haircutting ceremony takes place. In Namhalli, this ceremony usually involves the mother's brother or a substitute and the members of the household. Ear piercing, with or without a ceremony, is usually done during the first year and is required of all male and female children except Muslims for religious reasons.

For the first five years of its life, or until it is displaced by another child, the infant is fed on demand, picked up and carried whenever it cries, and generally treated as a pet. Consistent with the apparent policy of providing optimum conditions for survival, there are few attempts at discipline or training. The infant is wiped with rags when it defecates. Older children are taken outside and washed with water. There is little concern about toilet training. If weaning becomes necessary, the mother may smear her breast with a chili paste to discourage nursing. Usually the child nurses as long as milk is available. In general, the treatment of young children is tender and nurturant, the crying child immediately becoming the center of attention for any older children or adults within range of its voice. Nevertheless, children are not always comfortable. They are attacked by bedbugs, heat rash, and diarrhea, and they may protest bitterly when their mother departs to gather firewood or work in the fields.

With the birth of another baby, the acquisition of language skills, and the development of an ability to walk and to cope with the world generally, the infant gradually becomes what Margaret Mead has called a "yard child" rather than a house child. In Namhalli, children from the age of three begin following their older brothers and sisters to school. In Elephant and Gopalpur, where schooling carries few economic advantages, the yard children form play groups in which they pretend to undertake such activities as plowing and preparing food.

From the age of five or six, children are asked to perform such tasks as collecting cowdung, running errands to the store, bringing grass for the cattle, or herding cattle. Young children frequently run away or refuse to obey commands. Such behavior stimulates laughter at first, but if it continues, it leads to verbal abuse ("Donkey!" "May you eat mud!") and finally to beatings or starvation.

Especially in more traditional villages such as Elephant and Gopalpur, there is little further effort at child training. For the most part, children seem to welcome the opportunity to participate in adult activities, and they begin to help with agricultural and household work as soon as they are permitted and encouraged to do so. Many children appear at their houses only for eating and sleeping, and any control exerted on their behavior outdoors comes from older brothers and sisters, other playmates, or any adult who happens to be passing by. Children's play groups exist virtually unnoticed as part of the ambience of the village, but any adult will intervene immediately if one child strikes another or if play becomes dangerous.

In general, the need for a child and the quality of care and training a child receives depend on its birth order and sex. Early-born male children tend to receive the best care that can be provided. Inadequate resources or the injudicious use of existing resources results in far less adequate care for female and late-born children.

In the large extended family, especially if the older brother's wife exerts her influence, younger brothers and their families may have comparatively limited access to family resources.

Because ways of limiting family size—through abstention from sex, abortion, infanticide, or child neglect—are applied as a result of policies decided upon by the mother or the head of the household, it is inevitable that bad planning and tender-mindedness lead to raising excessive numbers of children in some households. One frequent result is a division of the family property in which each of the male children is left with lands inadequate for subsistence and funds inadequate for arranging marriages for all the male children.

Very often, especially in former times, this problem was met by accepting a loan, to be paid back by the labor of one of the male children. This sometimes amounts to a system of peonage, in which the young man works throughout his lifetime without earning enough money to pay more than the interest on the loan, but the more common practice is for the employer to provide the young man with funds for his marriage after a period of labor. In the Gopalpur region, a young man's period of service may be as short as one year; in the Namhalli region, it is often five years or more. Of course, funds for a young man's marriage may also be given in the form of a loan. In such cases, the period of service is extended indefinitely, and a few wealthy men in the Namhalli region are accused of having kept certain families in hereditary servitude by means of debts that continued from generation to generation.

"Skinflint" practices of this kind appear to be more common in the Namhalli region, as a consequence of a labor surplus that developed in the early stages of Namhalli's modernization and as a result of the fact that many of the "wealthy" families in the region are only marginally capable of supporting servants. In the Gopalpur region, with its rural aristocracy, the role of the wealthy patron-employer is much more clearly defined, and the public relations value of generosity is much greater than its costs. Traditional patterns of high mortality in the Gopalpur region, coupled in recent times with urban migration, have maintained a comparative shortage of agricultural labor, and this too provides an incentive for fair treatment of servants. In the Elephant region, few households can afford servants of any kind.

In some cases, the children of poor families leave voluntarily or are driven out. Another technique for coping with excess male children is to arrange their marriage with the daughters of wealthy men. In such cases, the young husband sets up a dependent household adjoining that of his father-in-law and receives compensation in land. Where the father-in-law has no sons, the son-in-law may be "adopted" and inherit the family property. Another way of acquiring a male child, more frequent in earlier times, is to dedicate a daughter to a local temple. The lovers of such dedicated women (*Basavis*) are expected to donate money to the temple, and the male offspring are raised as sons by the woman's father.

So far, the discussion has centered upon the role of family decision-making in determining the number of male and female children in the household. Where households fail for one reason or another to match their personnel to their resources, the time of reckoning comes when the children reach marriageable age. In high-ranking vegetarian jatis, where the parents of the bride are required to furnish large sums of money to arrange their daughters' marriages, the marriages of several daughters may impoverish a family. The brother of Gopalpur's Brahman Headman, who had five daughters, sold most of his property to arrange for their marriages. For lack of a dowry, some Brahman women never marry. The institution of dowry creates an equilibrating system in which surplus women are often unable to marry and are therefore unable to produce children. This institutional restriction on population growth, largely confined to high-ranking vegetarian jatis, seems to provide each newly formed household both with a "nest egg" and an incentive to produce relatively few children.

In jatis where the bride-price and other expenses are paid by the family of the groom, a shortage of funds may result in prolonged delays of the marriages of younger brothers. Such delays mean that the household remains intact over a longer period of time and thus acquires the benefit of a large staff of adult male workers. Where younger brothers insist on a household's division, their share of its possessions may be too small to permit marriage. More commonly, they succeed in marrying, but the resulting poverty severely limits their chances of producing many children. Households that produce large numbers of children of either sex labor at an economic disadvantage so great as to make it unlikely that the children will ever themselves be in a position to produce large numbers of children. Economic pressures and marriage rules favor the perpetuation of families that produce moderate numbers of children and are able to maintain a reasonable balance between the size of their agricultural holdings and the number of children who will inherit them. Due to infant mortality, the ideal of several sons and one or two daughters tends to result in a completed family that is somewhat smaller.

Short of marriage, family division, or other radical measures, there are a variety of ways of adjusting to permanent or temporary imbalances in household composition. Household labor needs can be met by flexible role assignments. If there is no older sister to care for a baby, the grandmother, grandfather, or even an older brother may be called upon to fill the role. If there is no small boy to care for the animals, a grandparent or daughter may assume the duty. For adults, such flexibility is more limited. Women never plow or undertake heavy agricultural operations, and men, while often competent to cook, almost never undertake to grind grain or perform other arduous tasks associated with food processing.

A household that lacks both an active adult male and an active adult female maintains itself only with the greatest difficulty. A single adult female can generally support herself—less often, her children—by begging, by renting out fields, by cooking and selling snacks, or by prostitution or concubinage. All of these occupations provide free time for such tasks as grinding grain or pounding rice. An adult male must generally support himself through farming or farm labor and is left without time to perform food processing tasks. Unless there is a daughter old enough to perform housework, households consisting of single adult males or single adult males and their children are practically nonexistent except in the city. A widowed adult male is constantly urged to remarry and often receives assistance for this purpose from his wife's family or from friends and neighbors.

The absence of needed family members, whether temporary or permanent, is also remedied by cooperation with other households. Child care may be provided by visisting relatives or neighbors. Cattle may be herded by a small boy or a grandparent from another household who is paid for his services. Where the adult male has more work than he can handle, a servant or relative may be imported more or less permanently to solve the problem. The wholesale importation of relatives was especially marked in Namhalli, where increasing access to factory jobs led to bringing poor relatives into the village to manage family lands that would otherwise have been abandoned.

Although the individual household provides most of the energy required to maintain the agricultural and population ecologies, it cannot meet all its needs for labor and manpower, and some must come from other households in the village. Even this is not enough. The village is inevitably dependent on other villages for goods and manpower. Thus, beyond the agricultural and population ecologies of the single village, there is a community ecology represented by the relationships between the individual village and the villages surrounding it. The chief agencies for the development and maintenance of community ecology are the system of jatis and the system of endogamous marriage within jatis. This is the topic of the next chapter.

Chapter 6

INTERVILLAGE RELATIONSHIPS: JATI AND MARRIAGE

The Brahman Headman of the village of Gopalpur owns about 200 acres, one-sixth of the village lands. The most valuable portion of this property is a shady garden and orchard located on the banks of the perennial stream that bisects the village lands. The heart of this old and well-established garden is a shrine dedicated to the Lingayat deity Basavanna. Proper attention must be paid to this deity if he is to continue to bless and sanctify the garden.

Because Basavanna is a Lingayat deity, it is essential that his image and shrine be tended not by a Brahman, such as the Headman, but by a Jangama or Lingayat priest. Some years ago, the Jangama responsible for the shrine ceased to tend it and it lay neglected. Because there were no resident Jangamas within the village, the Headman persuaded a poor Jangama from another village to sever his deep and long-established roots in that village and move to Gopalpur. The inducements, a house and five acres of land, were substantial, and a new household and jati were added to Gopalpur.

Although the coming of the Jangama had implications for the maintenance of Gopalpur's relationship with the natural environment and for the growth of village population, the priest was brought primarily to satisfy sacred obligations inherent in the South Indian world view. In addition, his presence was required also to maintain the prestige of Gopalpur's Headman and of the village itself in relation to other headmen and other villages. Although no one in Gopalpur would dispute the idea that neglect of the divine leads to divine neglect or even divine punishment, it is also true that no South Indian village would want to be known as a place where religion falters and dharma is absent.

The case of the migratory priest is a minor illustration of the point that an understanding of South Indian village ecology cannot be simply an understanding of the relationships that a village maintains with its immediate physical environment. Ordinarily a village cannot survive unless it produces crops and unless it reproduces its population. Equally, it cannot survive unless it maintains relationships with other villages. These relationships can be maintained only through reasonable adherence to the ways of life sanctioned by the South Indian world view, so that most of what happens in the village meets the approval of persons living elsewhere. Links with other villages permit the exchange of personnel, capital, technology, goods, and ideas, and therefore play an important part in influencing and regulating village population and agricultural production. This chapter deals with the system of jati and marriage that provides the framework for cooperation and exchange between villages.

The dharmic ideal of different jatis working together to form a single united and "self-sufficient" village was an important factor in bringing the Jangama priest to Gopalpur. This ideal of the multi-jati village encourages most villages to add jatis to the population as growing resources permit. There is a close correlation between the size of a village's population and the number of its jatis.

However, it is difficult for a small village to enable a variety of jatis to achieve an adequate income through the pursuit of their traditional occupation. With a smaller than desirable clientele, Gopalpur's Jangama priest is impoverished and must supplement his income by selling sacred cowdung ash and running a small private school. A few years ago, Gopalpur's 80 or 90 households were just adequate to support a single Barber. Unfortunately, Gopalpur's Barber had two sons. The consequences of this absence of family planning were overcome through the addition of the neighboring village of Gannapur to the family's inherited clientele. Now, Gopalpur's two Barbers each work part-time in Gopalpur, where both live, and part-time in Gannapur, which has no resident Barber.

The jati system makes it impossible for a single village to fulfill its need for occupational specialists by transferring members of the existing population from one job to another. Consequently, members of small specialized jatis, such as the Jangama and the Barbers, frequently move from village to village. Failing that, such specialists must arrange to obtain their clients in a number of villages. Many specialists in South Indian villages do not in fact work full-time at their trades and may derive a large part of their income from the ownership and management of farmland or from casual labor obtained during seasons of heavy agricultural work. For example, during the Gopalpur sowing and harvest seasons, when nobody has time for a regular shave and haircut, the two village Barbers earn income as agricultural laborers.

Although every village in the Gopalpur region requires the services of members of the Astrologer and Goldsmith jatis, the demand for these services is quite limited. An Astrologer's services are required on special occasions and on New Year's Day, when he reads predictions from the *Pancanga*, a traditional ceremonial calendar. In this case, the Astrologer lives in one village and visits six others on New Year's Day. He also visits clients in different villages in order to establish the auspicious moment for the completion of wedding ceremonies and to determine the astrological compatibility of the bride and groom. Although the Astrologer's calendrical knowledge and predictions are vital to Gopalpur's most basic adaptations, agriculture and population regulation, his services are obtainable only so long as the village preserves good relationships with other villages in its region.

Many centuries ago, Gopalpur's Goldsmiths offended a powerful deity, presumably by cheating him, and now they escape divine punishment only by avoiding permanent residence and spending all their income as soon as possible and in the place where they earn it. The Goldsmiths move in a circular orbit through Gopalpur and neighboring villages, remaining a few weeks in each and working and spending with contagious gaiety. Even without the goad of divine curses, other jatis also move through the region, catching snakes or antelope, selling children's toys, entertaining, and making appeals for charity. Although many of these services might not be considered essential, they contribute a great deal to the quality of life. Gopalpur's shepherd boys would survive if the manufacturers of shepherd's pipes failed to make their annual visit, but they would not survive as well or as happily. Shepherd boys in some countries manage to make their own pipes, but here the idea of jati gives rise to a specialized profession, and the adjustment of that profession to the size and location of its market constitutes a small portion of a vast network of interrelationships among neighboring and even distant communities.

Gopalpur, a relatively small village, is more dependent on its neighbors for essential services than are large settlements. A large village may be proportionately more self-sufficient but this is partly because it derives some of its self-sufficiency by providing services to neighboring villages. Although the village of Yelher, near Gopalpur, has several thousand households, its population is not large enough to permit the daily slaughter of animals for mutton. Such daily slaughter is made possible only because a large part of the Butchers' clientele comes from neighboring villages. Yelher also supports shops that obtain their customers from smaller nearby villages.

In summary, the concept of a village as a self-sufficient unity in which each resident jati contributes a vital economic and ritual function represents an unattainable ideal, which becomes scarcely more accessible when population increases and more and more specialist jatis are added. Far from leading to real self-sufficiency, the ideal leads to a situation in which the vital requirements of any one village can only be obtained through the development of social and economic ties with other villages. Elephant is relatively isolated and contains only one jati. This means that every essential service it obtains has to be secured from other and sometimes quite distant villages. Thus no village in South India can be regarded as truly isolated; all are hooked into a system of interrelationships.

The specialization of jati function is only the beginning of the story of relationships among villages, for in addition to its economic functions, the jati has some very important demographic consequences. Specifically, marriages must take place outside of the lineage, usually a patrilineage, and inside the jati or the intermarrying segment of the jati. The Gopalpur Barbers are both descendants of the same male ancestor. Since they are the only Barbers in Gopalpur, there is no way for them to marry unless they find eligible brides outside Gopalpur. Because Gopalpur's Barbers originally came from another location, some of the Barbers they locate in other villages will be members of their patrilineage. The Gopalpur Barbers cannot marry women from these families: the brides they select must be from another village *and* from another lineage.

Over most of South India, the principal means of keeping track of lineage membership is some sort of lineage organization. In Gopalpur, Namhalli, and Elephant, such an organization takes the form of a *mane devaru*, a lineage deity who has a shrine in a particular place and who must be worshiped regularly by all members of the lineage he represents. In Elephant, where in 1952 tigers, elephants, wild boars, and cheetahs still constituted real threats to crops and livestock, the village was awakened shortly after 3:00 A.M. on March 10th by the roaring of a "tiger." As the people poured recklessly into the village streets, they encountered Basappa, roaring like a tiger and attempting to bite and claw those who were trying to subdue him. Finally, the Priest appeared and "made him quiet." Basappa explained:

Every year, I go on pilgrimage to the Madesvara Hills. It is Heaven on earth. If there were water in the village well, I would have insisted that you come along with me to see the great God. As there was no water, I postponed my usual trip.

At about 3:00 A.M., when I was sleeping, I felt a tiger pounce on me. I do not know what happened after that. When I recovered, I saw nothing but my own people around me and my wife telling me that she had set aside a rupee as a donation to Madesvara.

After repeating the God's name, I took an oath that I would visit the temple as soon as possible for a "vision" of the God. Whenever my visit to Madesvara is delayed, the tiger comes in my dreams and presses me with his great paws and makes a huge noise. I feel that I am about to die and I become unconscious. That is how Madesvara makes me remember him.

Madesvara is Basappa's mane devaru, or "house god." Such a deity is charged with looking after all the members of a particular lineage. To obtain his help and to avoid punishment, regular visits to his temple are essential. During family crises, particularly illnesses, funds are set aside for the lineage deity, and in the event of recovery a visit to the temple is supposed to be made. In addition, special festivals in honor of lineage dieties are held every few years, and the attendance of all lineage brothers and sisters at these celebrations is considered desirable. Organization around a lineage deity and his temple is not universal in South India, but some comparable kind of lineage organization occurs almost everywhere.

The idea that lineage members are brothers and sisters—too closely related to marry each other—stems from a perception of human biology rooted in the South Indian world view. According to this view, a child derives its characteristics from only one parent. In patrilineal organizations this is usually explained in terms of the folk idea that the woman is merely the field in which the man sows his seed. Son and daughter are therefore biologically identical to the father, and all members of a lineage, because they are all descendants of the same male ancestor, are also biologically identical.

Because incest can lead to childlessness and other forms of supernatural punishment, it is to be avoided at all costs, and this is why marriage between members of the same lineage is absolutely forbidden and scrupulously avoided. Over the years, as lineages have risen and fallen and ancient ancestors have been forgotten, the lineage has ceased to contain all the "brothers" and "sisters" that a man might have. In many cases, quite different jatis are descended from the same deities or saints and may therefore contain unknown brothers and sisters. It is therefore extremely dangerous to marry any stranger who cannot be shown with certainty to be a member of a "safe" lineage within the same jati. A "safe" lineage is one with which numerous successful marriages have been contracted in the past. It is useful to view the jati for this purpose as consisting of parallel or similar lineages containing "brothers" and "sisters" and cross or complementary lineages containing potential spouses.

The organization of villages into jatis, many of which consist of only a few households, leads to a situation in which all members of some jatis in a single village belong to the same lineage. Even where this is not the case, quarrels between different lineages or the unavailability of suitable spouses from the same village compel at least half of all bridegrooms to seek brides in other villages. Within each village, agricultural production and child raising are dependent on the household. The household, in turn, is dependent on marriage, and marriage is dependent on a continuing exchange of spouses between villages. The household itself can be interpreted as a point of intersection between the social and economic organization of the village community and a marital organization represented by jatis and lineages.

To the extent that a household must choose between community imperatives and jati-lineage imperatives, it serves two masters. Behavior within the community and within the jati and lineage is restricted by the pressures which the jati and the community may bring to bear against each other. Open fighting between communities, between jatis, or between communities and jatis is not entirely unknown, but its severity and frequency are restricted and controlled by the division of household loyalties between them. A war between jatis is usually a war between members of the same community, and a war between communities is partly a war between members of the same jatis and lineages.

MARRIAGE

Marriage establishes the family household and serves to regulate relationships between communities and between lineages within the same jati. A successful marriage, where the husband and wife work well together and children are produced, is essential to every aspect of the ecological system. An understanding of the complicated technology underlying the choice of suitable spouses and the arrangement of marriage is fundamental to an understanding of the means by which village communities perpetuate themselves and cope with their environments.

Because the prevailing pattern of mariage is patrilocal, which means that the bride takes up residence in the household of the groom or his parents, much of the technology of marriage has to do with selecting a suitable bride and ensuring that she is satisfactory to the groom, to his household, and to his community. First, as described above, the bride and groom must be properly related: the marriage must not be incestuous. Equally important, the bride must be of "good character." The most common and obvious implication of this complicated concept is that the bride should be a virgin at the time of marriage and should avoid men other than her husband following the marriage. Further implications include a sentiment that the bride is a dangerous external element introduced into the body of the household and village. Should she or her habits prove to be unclean or polluting, the consequences for husband, household, and village could be serious.

The idea that danger is associated with women is reflected in the existence of disease goddesses who are the source of deadly epidemics. It is also related to the belief that males and penises can be cleansed of pollution while females and vaginas cannot. Pollution is the obverse of the spiritual and physical purity required for the achievement of enlightenment. It results from unclean acts, impure thoughts, or simply from commingling substances which should be kept apart. A woman may cause a man to release his semen rather than store it up as a source of spiritual power. She involves him in the mundane concerns of parenthood. If she is careless with her menstrual blood, her husband may sicken and fruit trees in the village may die. She may poison her husband, or more likely her mother-in-law, by adding deadly or impure substances to the food they eat. A wife who lacks a "good character" may foment quarrels between brothers which cause family division.

In view of the manifold real and supernatural dangers involved in bringing in a new bride, every community and jati in South India possesses complicated techniques and rules designed to ensure proper bride selection. In Namhalli and Elephant, the first line of defense is to arrange as many marriages as possible within the village. In the absence of a suitable bride within the village, one is sought in closely neighboring villages or in villages with which many successful marriages have been arranged in the past. These options are not always available to the members of small and scattered jatis. Even where spouses are available within the village or within closely neighboring villages, there may be compelling social or economic reasons for attempting marriages with comparative strangers. In Namhalli, which serves as an important link between the city and the rural hinterland, heads of families often seek to arrange marriages with potential trading partners in the city or in the hinterland. Wealthy families, which tend to place great emphasis on family unity and the subservience of their women, may seek brides from poor families and distant places on the theory that such brides, lacking the support of kinsmen, can be easily controlled.

Yeoman farmers, who make up an overwhelming majority of the three villages discussed here, generally have a compelling interest in importing women who will not cause trouble either in the super-natural realm of pollution or in the natural realms of infidelity, family disputation, and laziness. These risks are believed to be best avoided by obtaining the new bride from the same source from which previous brides have been obtained; that is, by marrying a close relative. Assuming, as is the case for all except the very highest-ranking vegetarian jatis, that it is the groom's family that seeks the bride, the most desirable bride is the closest possible rela-tion who cannot conceivably belong to the same lineage as the groom. There are, in fact, three ideal marriages: mother's brother's daughter, father's sister's daughter, and sister's daughter.

In these three cases, the marriage cannot possibly be incestuous because the bride belongs to her *father's* lineage, which is a "safe" lineage as demonstrated by her father's fertile and successful mar-riage. Marriage to such close relatives has advantages other than avoiding incest. Relationships between brothers and sisters living in neighboring villages are generally very close, and usually the brother visits his sister frequently and looks after her interests. It is logical to reaffirm this close relationship by arranging a mar-riage between oneself or one's son and the daughter of a brother or sister. It is also logical to assume, though this doesn't always work out in practice, that a favorite niece or granddaughter will support the bridegroom's parents and will have the best possible training and character. From the other side, the parents of the bride have every assurance that their daughter will be well treated.

Although marriage to close relatives is generally justified in terms of family sentiment and the avoidance of incest, it is also believed that such marriages have significant practical advantages. Of these, the most important is that a close relative will not demand family division. Marriage among close relatives is therefore thought to strengthen and probably does strengthen the extended joint family household, thus permitting more efficient use of economic and political resources. Such marriages may also be cheaper to arrange, and, because they are considered more stable, may tend to prevent costly marital disputes and remarriages.

Although it is feasible to construct mathematical models per-mitting an estimate of the maximum proportion of close relative marriages that would take place under ideal conditions, no way has been found to apply such estimates to real life. In Elephant, where 49 percent of all existing marriages in 1952 were with close relatives, it appears probable that almost all possible marriages of this kind had been achieved. In Gopalpur and Namhalli, where the proportions were 21 and 33 percent, respectively, it can be concluded that many households had not arranged marriages with close relatives.

One reason for the high incidence of close relative marriage in Elephant is that the pool from which prospective brides can be chosen is quite small. Because so many marriages take place within Elephant or between residents of Elephant and a few neighboring villages, it is difficult to find a prospective bride who is *not* a close relative. In Gopalpur and Namhalli, the relatively small size of each village jati makes it difficult to marry within the village. There must be a relatively high proportion of marriages outside the village, and because there are a large number of neighboring villages, the pool from which brides are chosen is large and contains many persons whose relationships are distant or unknown.

Family heads in Namhalli and Gopalpur are also likely to be engaged in trade or other activities that make it economically and politically advisable to have many relatives in the surrounding villages. Typically, the oldest son may be married to a close relative and the younger sons to distant relatives or strangers in villages with which the family has had no previous ties. Thus marriage is in effect used to create a network of kinsmen in the neighboring villages. Such a network may be used to secure access to powerful men who can be helpful in obtaining loans or jobs, or to establish trading partners, and sources of labor. Close relative marriage is a means of continuing and strengthening an existing relationship. Marriage to new relatives may represent the abandonment of a previous set of kinship ties, but more often it represents an expansion of the network of kinsmen upon whom the family can call in case of need.

This ramified web of relationships creates a situation in which any person visiting another village for the first time can quickly establish his credentials by identifying his own jati and village. If his jati is represented in the village, at least one of his close relatives is likely to be present. If his jati is absent, he is still likely to encounter a woman from his own village or a close relative of one of his friends or neighbors. Elephant and its tiny region reflect an ancient and well-established pattern of rural isolation. However, other parts of South India have for centuries consisted of tightly integrated rural regions containing hundreds of thousands of persons interrelated through a network of marriages. In effect, rural South India combines the bigness of the city and the lack of anonymity of the small town. It is thus easy to travel from village to village and easy to find known and trustworthy people with whom to stay and to do business. The confident ease of people in strange places is summed up in the following anecdote, related by a Namhalli Shepherd:

On the day before yesterday, in the morning, I went to another village to my friend's house. My friend's younger brother has to marry this year. My friend asked me to go with him to a third village where a fellow Flower Gardener is reported to have a marriageable daughter. We wanted to meet this man and ask him indirectly what he thought about the idea of giving his daughter to my friend's brother. We wanted to study him, his wealth and his manners.

We reached the village at 6:00 P.M. and went to his house. He offered us food and shelter. First, we asked him whether seed potatoes were available. He told us that he could procure them for us. The next morning, he took us to his garden, where he has a number of vegetables. We met his neighbors and heard about the girl's character and the crops grown by the family.

By afternoon, our host had realized that we had not come for seed potatoes. He told us that he would visit my friend's village in a short time. We gladly accepted and asked him to visit it as soon as possible. He undoubtedly wants to view all details as we did in his village.

After examining our host's situation, we felt that he was neither rich nor poor. He has four male and four female children; none are married. All of them are working in the garden, the rice paddies, and the dry lands. All year round he has some crops growing in his garden. He has four milk cows, a number of goats, and a pair of bullocks in his house. He has an iron safe, some big vessels, and a good grain storer. A few days back, they sold potatoes for 500 rupees. Now they have another crop of potatoes ready for picking.

My friend told me that he thought our host wanted to arrange for an exchange of daughters. As my friend has no readily marriageable daughters, he plans to show one of his relatives' daughters to our host. My friend has a father's brother who has two marriageable daughters.

In addition to the obvious adaptive advantages conferred by this easy method of establishing friendships and relationships among villages, the system of marriage has the important effect of regulating the movement of persons and thereby regulating the population of individual villages. This process works in several ways, but primarily by determining who shall be married and under what sort of economic circumstances. For most middle-ranking and low-ranking jatis, the bridegroom's family must possess substantial sums of money to arrange a marriage. Where the family is poor, or where it possesses many sons, the potential bridegroom must often leave the community in search of work. If he is successful in finding work and saving money, he will return later to be married. Those who are unsuccessful tend never to return, falling victim to malnutrition and disease or becoming part of India's hopeless and largely male urban poor.

Even when a poor man does succeed in acquiring the necessary funds, he may still be unable to arrange a completely satisfactory marriage. Regardless of his age, he must marry a bride who has not yet reached puberty. Even in Namhalli, where there is a tendency to stretch things a bit, this means that the bride cannot be more than 16 years old. The longer it takes the bridegroom to assemble funds for his marriage, the greater the discrepancy in age between the bride and the groom. Biologically speaking, a woman can have just as many children with an older male as with a younger, but in practice large age discrepancies between bride and groom often result in unsatisfactory marital relationships and divorce. Finally, the bridegroom who cannot easily afford to get married may find that once married, he cannot afford to provide adequately for his wife and children.

The effects of marriage rules and other constraints on the demographic fortunes of the poor are complicated, and there are no typical cases. The following incident, which could have occurred anywhere in South India, expresses one aspect of the situation:

There was a man of this village who was married to B's daughter. After his marriage he was given the job of grazing sheep. He had two children. His wife and both children became pale and thin and died. After they died, he would go to the garden and wander without food. After four years, he married a woman from C. She was in his house for about two years, but left because the father-in-law and brother-in-law were making trouble. They made her go away. After she had gone, he didn't know what to do. From that day, his brother and father made him work hard. They were not giving him food at mealtime. They were harvesting him without food. This was about four days back when he was plowing. He had not had any food or water for about two days. He became depressed. He went to the garden by himself and then returned home. At about 5:00 P.M. he went to the garden and threw himself into the well. His name was G, and his age was fifty years.

Another option, almost as unsatisfactory, that is available to poor bridegrooms is to marry a comparatively wealthy bride and go to live in her village. In such a case, the bridegroom is usually given lands adequate to support him and his family. In return, he isolates himself from his friends and relatives and spends the rest of his life under the thumbs of his wife and her family. In a patrilineal, patrilocal, and patriarchal society, he faces the special contempt reserved for the unmanly male. On the other hand, he eats well and, in the event that his father-in-law has no sons, he may inherit substantial wealth. In Gopalpur, where most families are poor and where a population shortage has only recently begun to develop as a result of migration to Bombay, such matrilocal marriages do not occur. In Elephant, where surpluses of land sometimes develop, the proportion of matrilocal marriages reaches 3 percent. In Namhalli, where many locally born males commute to work in the nearby telephone factory, a pressing shortage of manpower has forced the rate of matrilocal marriage up to 9 percent. In other words, when there is a shortage of population, individual families in a village tend to increase their wealth to a point where they can contemplate the large expense of arranging matrilocal marriages for their daughters. With both sons and daughters remaining in the village and bringing in their wives and husbands, the population of the village increases until an ecological balance is established and decreasing numbers of families can afford such marriages.

The three basic kinds of close relative marriage (that is, to mother's brother's daughter, father's sister's daughter, and sister's daughter) imply three different kinds of exchange between villages. Mother's brother's daughters involve a form of marriage in which the son obtains his bride from the same village in which his father obtained his own bride. In population terms, this means a series of marriages in which women are transferred from Village B to Village A, but not in the reverse direction. Cash, in the form of bride-price or marriage expenses, moves from Village A to Village B. This type of marriage generally carries the implication that the bride and her family are of lower social and economic status than the bridegroom and his family. If Village B obtains its brides from Village C and so on until the nth village is reached, a chain of villages of progressively lower status is created. The nth village, which would be extremely poor, would have no place to obtain brides, and its young men would be forced to migrate, often as a result of matrilocal marriages.

The clearest example of this process is found among the Namhalli Blacksmiths, who obtain brides from a distant and isolated village and tend to give brides to nearby towns and cities. Because the Namhalli Blacksmiths are almost all employed by the telephone company, they have tended to import male relatives of their wives and mothers to perform necessary chores in the local fields and smithies. Many of these relatives have migrated to Namhalli as a result of matrilocal marriages. The demographic effect of this pattern is to increase the population of Namhalli and to decrease the population of the distant village. Given unlimited growth of the telephone company, which would provide a constantly expanding resource base for Namhalli, this process could result in depopulation of the rural village. Assuming limits to the growth of Namhalli, the process would have the long-term effect of equalizing the ratio of population to resources and hence would lead to greater economic equality of the two villages.

Sister's daughter and father's sister's daughter marriages involve a pattern of exchange of women between two villages either within the same generation or with a one-generation delay. Father's sister is given to Village B, and one generation later the gift is returned in the form of her daughter; sister is given to Village B, and her daughter is returned within a few years. A more immediate return takes place when men exchange sisters as brides. All of these forms of exchange imply an absolute equality between the two households and a substantial reduction in the cost of marriage. Exchange marriages do not have any direct demographic effects, but because each side holds the other's daughter hostage, they tend to ensure proper treatment of the bride. This contributes to the stability of such marriages and to the perpetuation of extended family organizations.

So far, the discussion has emphasized the ways in which the bride is selected and their various demonstrable and problematic effects. Once a likely prospect has been identified as a possible bride, a complex process of investigation and negotiation is insti-

tuted. As illustrated in the quotation on page 117, the process begins with a visit of the bridegroom's parents to the bride's parents.
Following this, both sets of parents make a series of visits to each
other's villages. Each time they do so, gifts are exchanged, expenses
are incurred, and promises are given. The pattern is thus one of
progressively deepening commitment to the establishment of a
relationship between the two families.

Each step of this deepening commitment involves the performance of public ceremonial. On each visit, the guests are taken in
procession through the village and the hosts distribute food to both
invited and uninvited guests. The success of the religious ceremonial attached to each stage of the arrangements depends on
the willingness of all persons in the village to participate.

As arrangements are completed and the time of the marriage ap-
proaches, the dependence of the groom's family (in whose house
the marriage occurs) on other persons in the village becomes increasingly formal. If the wedding is to take place, representatives
of all the important jatis must agree to play official and stereotyped
roles. For example, in Namhalli, low-ranking Leatherworkers must
construct the outdoor booth within which the ceremony will take
place. The Barber and the Leatherworker must play the pipe and
drum for the ceremony; the Washerman must bring clean saris to
form a carpet for the bride and groom to walk upon. The Goldsmith
must prepare the wedding jewelry, and a Brahman or Jangama
priest, depending on the bridegroom's jati, must conduct the
ceremony.

In addition to functionaries drawn from different jatis, all village
leaders and important men must be present or represented by
members of their families. It is desirable that representatives of
important religious shrines and other regionally important persons
and as many relatives of the bride and groom as possible also be
present. Ideally, the wedding should be attended by the head of
every household in the village.

If conflicts exist between the households of the bride and groom
and any of the jatis, officials, neighbors, important men, or relatives
who are expected to participate in the wedding, or if any of these
persons believe the wedding should not take place, they may signify their displeasure by refusing to attend, to perform their official
functions, or to accept the offerings of food and cash that are

normally their due. When this happens, there is a stir of conversation among the wedding guests as they relay the information that the Barber is sitting in his house refusing to attend, that a Mother's Brother has angrily departed, or that a creditor is demanding payment before he will participate. After a period of stunned inaction, one of the important guests, perhaps a Big Man from a neighboring village, demands that the nonparticipant be brought before the assembled men of importance. Soon he appears, wearing a sheepish look, and states his case. Perhaps the Barber protests not having received his annual allotment of grain, and the groom's father argues that this was because he had lost or stolen a shirt. Perhaps the Mother's Brother argues that the groom should marry his daughter rather than the chosen bride, and the groom's father counters by saying that the Mother's Brother gave his own son in marriage to another household. As the debate goes on, the important men—to say nothing of the wedding party—become increasingly tired, hungry, and impatient. Threats are used to mobilize a spirit of compromise, and the disputants finally agree to a settlement. The dark cloud of conflict now dissipates, and the participants resume the compulsory good cheer and friendliness characteristic of religious festivities.

In effect, then, the marriage takes place with the unanimous consent and goodwill of all persons in the villages of both bride and groom and very frequently of various personages from the surrounding region. When a village is rent by irreconcilable conflicts, there is grave danger that weddings and all other religious ceremonials will cease to be conducted. It is especially at the time of a marriage that the important men of the region exert strong punitive sanctions—halting the marriage, for example—against the members of a village that has failed to maintain dharma. If weddings are to be held at all, the members of a quarrelsome village must resolve their differences at least long enough to permit them to take place. Weddings are the most important and most lavish ceremonies held in any South Indian village. Not only do they affirm and reaffirm linkages among neighboring villages, but they also ameliorate and resolve conflicts within villages. Perhaps even more important, they encourage the wise man, with his well-regulated household, to observe dharma in his relationships with others and thereby to ensure that the weddings held in his household will not be disrupted by conflict.

In this chapter I have described the nature of the relationships among villages established through jati and marriage. The division of villages into jatis and of jatis into lineages leads to the formation of organizations that cut across the local community. Because these organizations are vitally concerned with the arrangement of marriages and because marriages must take place within jatis and between lineages, the completion of marital arrangements results in the construction of complicated systems of relationships among neighboring communities. All villages and towns within a region are directly connected with one another through membership in the same lineages and jatis and through the relationships established by marriage. Because marriage involves the movement of individuals from one village to another, it also has implications for the adjustment of village populations to available resources. The need to arrange marriages between persons living in different villages permits influence to be exerted on any particular village. Such influence is used to bring errant villages into conformity with the patterns of life sanctioned by the South Indian world view, and it is expressed most directly through threats to the harmony and cooperation required in the conduct of the marriage ceremony. Taken together, the system of jati and marriage provides a series of pathways between communities along which other important relationships, to be described in the following chapters, can take place.

Chapter 7

INTERVILLAGE RELATIONSHIPS: ECONOMIC EXCHANGE

In South India, the night holds many terrors, and these are multiplied in proportion to distance from the nearest human habitation. Evil spirits may possess a wayward traveler, driving him insane or killing him. Tigers and snakes, often imaginary, leap aggressively out of the bushes or lurk ominously along the trail. Bandit gangs or practitioners of human sacrifice are often seen or heard in the darkness. In the daytime, these real and imaginary dangers disappear. Small children wander freely from village to village, and the unarmed traveler walks with light, unworried step.

Violent death may occur as a result of confrontations between the residents of neighboring villages or of quarrels among inhabitants of the same village, but even in traditional times, when bandits did indeed lurk in gullies and secret places, death at the hands of a stranger was relatively rare. During wars among states and principalities, the ordinary villager plowed his fields, traveled to markets or pilgrimage centers, and carried out marital arrangements with little concern for the activities of the "great people" whose bloody battles might be raging only a few miles away.

Although depictions of rural South India as a place of bucolic harmony, goodwill, and dharma are sometimes exaggerations reflecting the high ideals of the South Indian world view rather than the realities, the South Indian villager is more accepting of his neighbors and less hostile to strangers than are village-dwelling people elsewhere in the world. This can be attributed in part to the system of jati and marriage, which ensures the constant interchange of inhabitants among villages and throughout regions.

Rural harmony is also fortified by market systems that permit economic exchange between villages, by common religious organizations and worship, and, especially in recent times, by an organized and bureaucratic government. These three modes of integration are independent neither of one another nor of the system of jati and marriage. The market system is deeply affected by the association of particular occupations and activities with jati membership and by the personal relationships established through shared membership and intermarriage. Major religious shrines and organizations are generally connected with specific jatis, and the conduct of ceremonies requires the specialized participation of a variety of jatis. Although the concept of an impartial and impersonal government bureaucracy is by no means absent in South India, kinship, jati membership, and religious sects deeply affect governmental processes.

South Indian systems of trade and marketing, involving the exchange of labor, goods, and capital, reflect the fact that no South Indian village has to produce all that it consumes or consume all that it produces. Basic economic decisions concerning agricultural production are made within the farmer's household. Decisions on the planting of particular crops involve evaluations of the potentialities of the farmer's lands, skills, household needs (it is usually cheaper to grow your own food), and of the probable market price of the ultimate crops. Because this price depends on regional, national, and even international supply and demand, the determining effect of environment and technology on the choice of crops is modified by the farmer's knowledge of the crops likely to be grown elsewhere. A farmer who has difficulty producing onions may nevertheless raise them in order to utilize surplus labor in his household or because he thinks there will be a greater than usual demand for them. Very often, when high demand is expected, a crop will be planted by too many hopeful farmers, and a glut will result.

Although most farmers lay their plans rationally and thoughtfully, records of a kind that would permit any very exact computation of profit and loss are rarely kept. There is a tendency to plant familiar crops year after year on the assumption that if they don't sell this year, they will sell next year. Gopalpur, Namhalli, and Elephant have traditionally been villages which raise primarily subsistence crops. Modern Namhalli has specialized increasingly in the production of fruit and vegetable crops, but most of its farmers still emphasize the production of food for their own families. Although the predominant pattern of South Indian agriculture is one of subsistence farming complemented by small cash crops, many villages are relatively specialized and therefore trade cash crops for food crops. Near Gopalpur is the village of Chintanhalli, which has an abundant supply of water and specializes in betel leaves. The village of Balacakra, which has a sandy and infertile soil and a good supply of water, specializes in sweet potatoes. Although few villages practice one-crop farming and most villages raise a substantial proportion of food crops for domestic consumption, some villages can be regarded as practicing subsistence agriculture, others as engaged primarily in commercial farming. Some jatis—for example, the Toddy Tappers, who obtain palm beer— have highly specialized agricultural functions as their karma and react to market conditions slowly and painfully.

For a variety of reasons—some traditional, some ecological, and some based on market conditions—different villages tend to raise somewhat different crops. As described in the previous chapter, villages also tend to differ in jati composition, and this too leads to village specialization in particular goods and services. Single-crop villages, where agriculture can only be practiced during five or six months out of the year, may also develop specialized nonagricultural forms of production. Thus, stringed instruments of certain kinds are known to be manufactured only in a village some 40 miles northeast of Gopalpur. Another village, 60 miles southeast, specializes in the construction and repair of temples. Gopalpur's Stoneworkers, who possess very little high-quality land, spend much of their time away from the village, engaged in road building and other construction projects.

An effective system for the exchange of goods and services between villages is thus of considerable adaptive significance. It permits each village to grow the crops most suited to its unique ecological niche, and it enables the residents of agriculturally unproductive villages to supplement their income by providing other sorts of goods and services.

Taken together, patterns of exchange reaching across a given region constitute a market regulated by traditional concepts of dharma. Most buyers and sellers operate in the belief that the price of any particular good or service is permanently fixed by divine mandate in the same way that the ranks of different jatis are fixed. If there is an increase in price, it must be explained by the seller, and if the explanation is not satisfactory, a boycott is the automatic response. Another reason for this is that the buyer is invariably interrogated in detail when he returns to his home village. If he returns with inferior or overpriced merchandise, he is the victim of caustic criticism, and his crime may never be forgiven or forgotten. This kind of criticism extends to all kinds of economic relationships; one of Namhalli's more prosperous citizens always began his reminiscences by saying, "My father's older brother [the household head] was a fool; he used to give loans to anyone who asked for them."

When short supply and high demand bring extraordinary pressures to bear on the traditionally established value of some good or service, its price tends to rise slowly and only after agonizing debate. During World War II, an increasing demand for the services of Namhalli's Blacksmiths led to an increase in their charges only after the matter had been thoroughly discussed by the village council. Most individuals, heads of households especially, are aware of the price paid for every article in their possession. They know where almost any article can be purchased most cheaply, and they are pleased to quote the price that obtained in 1935 and to discuss in detail any changes in price that have taken place since. But in spite of this concern with prices, the farmer rarely calculates the cost of his own labor or that of his family and gives little consideration to the larger profits that might have been gained through alternative endeavors.

In sum, the production and exchange of goods and services cannot be interpreted as a purely rational activity. The farmer does not always choose to grow the crop best suited to his lands, and the price of what he grows is not always determined by the balance of supply and demand. In the long run, the system of exchange between villages tends to be self-correcting. Farmers who plant cash crops that can't be grown or can't be sold at a profit are likely to go out of business. When the individual farmer is primarily a subsistence farmer, as is generally the case in South India, his blunders in the production and distribution of his cash crops tend to be of marginal significance. The inefficient onion grower receives less cash than he would if he grew a more suitable crop, but he may still earn enough to satisfy his household needs. Individual households, particularly large ones, generally engage in a wide range of productive activities, including common labor, the performance of specialities unique to their jati, the raising of several kinds of irrigated and unirrigated grain and garden crops, and the breeding and feeding of several kinds of livestock. Such a wide dispersion of family activities contributes to the efficient utilization of the available manpower and limits the household's dependence on any particular crop or activity, but it makes any close calculation of costs and benefits practically impossible.

Although rice and garden crops, especially those that benefit from large and well-designed irrigation works, have a predictable yield from year to year, the yield of millet and other rain-fed crops is variable and unpredictable. As a result, farmers who study all relevant factors before planting may be little better off than the rest. Protection against unforeseen fluctuations in crop yields or in market conditions is generally obtained by borrowing grain and cash. Although a popular mythology among urban Indians and foreigners holds the moneylender responsible for much of South Indian rural poverty, most moneylenders will extend loans only to persons with substantial assets. Most poor people are free of debt because they cannot obtain loans except under some form of peonage.

Yeoman farmers, on the other hand, tend to borrow as much and as often as possible. In traditional times, and to a very considerable extent in modern times as well, the act of borrowing created an unbreakable bond between the patron moneylender and his client borrower. In the Gopalpur region, the borrower obtains seed grain and whatever grain and cash is required to support his household through the year. In return, he gives back double the amount of seed grain, assists with his patron's harvest, and pays between 12 and 18 percent interest at harvesttime.

In Gopalpur, the borrower is also expected to display loyalty and gratitude to the lender and is likely to be severly beaten if he fails to support his patron in disputes. At times of crop failure, or when the borrower incurs extraordinary expenses, such as outlays for a marriage, the patron is expected to increase the loan and waive interest. Because the patron himself is often in debt to wealthier men from large villages and towns, the pattern of patron-client relationships can be regarded as providing an underlying structure to economic relationships throughout the Gopalpur region. This structure is important in linking hamlets and small villages to large villages and in determining the nature of political alliances even at the state level. Especially at the upper levels, the hierarchy of economic relationships tends to be shrouded in secrecy.

Patron-client relationships are considerably less important in Elephant, where most people are too poor to borrow money. In Namhalli, wholesale importations of cash by factory workers have largely destroyed traditional patron-client relationships, and moneylenders tend to be more businesslike and impersonal.

South Indian marketing practices—exchanges of goods and services—are complex. For example, the wives and children of produce growers from nearby villages come to Gopalpur in the early morning hours with their tiny hoards of eggplant, tomatoes, greens, sweet potatoes, chilies, or mangoes. If these goods are sold in Gopalpur, the sellers return home; otherwise, they move on to a neighboring village, ultimately returning with a few handfuls of grain or the equivalent in copper coins.

A little later in the day, a *dasarayya* (religious minstrel) comes from his home village to pay his monthly visit to Gopalpur. At each household, he sings a song or two and receives a few coins in exchange. A betel leaf seller from a nearby hill village brings packets of leaves, which she drops off with one or two housewives who will resell them, a few leaves at a time, to every household in the village. During the day, especially if a successful harvest has been completed, a variety of beggars and performers may stream through. Some of them go from house to house, receiving a small gift of grain from each; others attract a crowd and collect gifts from the audience.

On other days, the Potter from a neighboring village may bring a cartload of his wares. Because Gopalpur has no resident Potter of its own to be paid on an annual jajmani basis, the pots are paid for individually as purchased. Again, following their annual schedule, the Goldsmiths may come to Gopalpur, camping in front of a Muslim shrine until they have exhausted the local demand for jewelry.

Several times daily, each household sends one of its children to the village store with a bit of grain or cash to trade for leaf-wrapped cigarettes, matches, or tiny portions of salt, sugar, spices, soap, cooking oil, or kerosene. These supplies are brought from the regional market in Yadgiri by the storekeeper, who travels the 12-mile distance each week with his cart.

Perhaps once a month, household representatives will visit the Sunday market at Kandkur, four miles away. Because items sold at the market are taxed, most people do not sell their produce there; rather, they buy the various items that professional vendors bring from town or regional markets. Most of the goods sold at the Kandkur market are imperishable: hand mirrors, combs, children's toys, utensils, cheap cloth, and ready-made clothing. Sometimes a few rubbery carrots or dilapidated potatoes are brought in. Occasionally a fair amount of local produce is available, but the dry air and high temperatures of the region generally make it necessary to transfer perishable goods directly from the seller to the buyer.

Near Namhalli, where raising produce is of much greater economic importance due to proximity to the city of Bangalore and better growing conditions, the local market has a tropical profusion of locally produced fruits and vegetables. Because the city is close to Namhalli and the bus service excellent, it is easier for family heads to buy imperishable goods directly from the city than in local markets. Village stores and local and regional markets near Namhalli carry a wider range of products than those near Gopalpur, reflecting relatively greater consumption on the part of their urbanized and educated consumers. At the same time, the relative importance of local economic networks is diminished by the ease of access to cheaper and better urban markets and shops.

Elephant, isolated from its nearest neighbors by considerable distances and mountain trails, follows a marketing pattern resembling that of Gopalpur but involving less consumption. Lacking shops of any kind, people in Elephant make weekly trips to the nearby market in the valley below. Even there, they buy and consume relatively little—pots for cooking, the cheapest cloth, a few fruits and vegetables.

Patterns for the trading of cattle also reflect environmental differences among the three villages. In the Gopalpur region, ecological circumstances do not favor cattle breeding. Cattle represent a major investment, and their purchase is carefully negotiated by earnest committees of village elders. Cows and female water buffalo are treasured sources of the clarified butter and milk required for the survival of infants, but the cows give very little of either. By contrast, Namhalli and Elephant are located at higher altitudes where cattle breed well and provide abundant milk. Elephant, because it is isolated, disposes of its surplus cattle to traveling merchants who buy the animals for sale in the cattle-short lowlands. In Namhalli, every farmer derives part of his income from breeding or training cattle. In the spring, the farmer purchases a small pair of bullocks which he uses for his plowing. When the millet fields are ripening, he has his son cut sugar-filled sorghum stalks daily and sits hour after hour hand-feeding his bullocks. When they are fat and healthy, the farmer drives them in gentle stages to a cattle fair, perhaps 20 or 30 miles away, and sells them at a substantial profit. In modern times, both Elephant and Namhalli have become involved in the supply of milk to the city of Bangalore.

For all three villages, the major economic events of the year are the harvests of the important millet and rice crops. In all three, the crop is heaped on the farmer's threshing ground and then divided among his creditors. Traditionally, the government collected its share of the harvest at that time and the remaining grain was stored by the farmer or his patron, often in underground pits of the kind still used in Elephant. More recently, the need to pay land taxes in cash and to acquire various newly introduced products has impelled the farmer to sell an increasingly large proportion of his crop. Because of rationing and price control, this often involves transporting the crop either to the city or a regional market, where it is sold for cash. Because Elephant lacks carts and, more important, cart roads, much of its grain must be stored. The resulting surplus of grain and lack of cash does much to explain the lack of consumer goods in Elephant. Poor people in Gopalpur and Namhalli often go hungry; people in Elephant are well fed even in famine years, but they possess few manufactured goods or luxury food items.

Overall, the system of economic relationships is one of direct exchange between households in different villages. Such exchange is facilitated and made possible by the existence of jati and kinship ties and by adherence to a common cultural tradition which defines dharmic relationships between buyers and sellers and contributes to the stability of prices. Direct exchange between villages, which, as discussed in previous chapters, also involves the exchange of labor, is of ecological significance because it permits individual villages and farmers to specialize in crops particularly suited to local microenvironments. Crudely stated, two villages, one of which grows rice and the other millet, are likely to represent a more stable and effective adaptation than are two villages that raise precisely the same crops. Within environmental limitations, agricultural specialization encourages the development of patterns of exchange and these patterns encourage agricultural specialization. The presence of different crops ripening at different times facilitates the sharing of a common work force among farmers and between villages.

Although crops intended for exchange between villages, especially produce, are not unimportant nutritionally, their economic significance is considerably less than that of staple food crops such as rice and millet, which are raised wherever possible. Because the millets are both cheaper and more nutritious than rice, the latter is often raised as a cash crop while the farmer subsists on the former. For most farmers and most villages, about half to one third of the grain crop remains in the village to be consumed by its households. The rest of the crop constitutes the energy resource that supports the populations of the towns and cities of South India. In traditional times, the bulk of this resource was obtained from villages through the collection of taxes, interest on loans, or rent charges paid to wealthy landholders. Relatively small amounts went to the support of regional and urban religious institutions. In modern times, the quantity of grain obtained through taxation has steadily declined, but equal or larger quantities now reach the city in exchange for manufactured goods ranging from soap to transistor radios.

The village is related to town and city through a vertical system of relationships in which urban goods move downward from city to town to local market or village store while grain moves upward from town to city, often passing through the hands of wealthy landlords and patrons on its way. Local exchange moves horizontally and informally in complex networks, as individual farmers and craftsmen produce their goods and exchange them directly with farmers and craftsmen living in other villages.

At a superficial level of analysis, it appears that systems of local exchange contribute much to the enrichment of life and adaptation to the environment, while (especially in traditional times) vertical exchanges contribute relatively little to the village. Even today, it is plain that the farmer loses more to taxes, interest, and price control than he receives in cash, government services, and manufactured goods. On the other hand, in both traditional and modern times, the farmer's security of life and many aspects of his technology have depended on the existence of political and religious institutions that could only be supported in towns and cities. The South Indian world view, which could only be the product of a literate urban civilization, provides the rationale for the farmer's life and sets the stage for productive cooperation and exchange both within and between villages. Although warfare among South Indian kingdoms has sometimes had devastating effects on the countryside, it is reasonable to conclude that the governments established in towns and cities removed much of the burden of self-defense from the rural communities and made possible the development of advantageous patterns of local exchange between villages. Problems of adaptation and accommodation between local villages and government officials are discussed in the following chapter.

Chapter 8

THE GOVERNMENT AND THE VILLAGE

According to the South Indian world view, the responsibility for regulating economic and political relationships between villages and among villages, towns, and cities falls to the *raja*, or ruler. The ruler, who should be a member of a warrior jati, is charged with responsibility for the relationships between jatis, for collecting taxes, and for regulating rents and interest charges. Because all of these obligations are specified in appropriate scriptures, the duty of the raja can be summed up as enforcing dharma within the kingdom. As a warrior, he is also obligated to defend and extend the boundaries of his kingdom. Conquest usually involved the subjugation of other rajas, who thereafter paid tribute to whoever succeeded in becoming a *maharaja,* or great raja. Especially in the more rugged parts of South India, the traditional raja was not always effective in preventing banditry or internal warfare. When dharma was properly enforced by the raja, the people were said to be happy and the countryside peaceful. The good king protected his people from abuse, but he was not expected to engage in many positive acts of assistance, such as famine relief, hospital construction, or building schools.

Present-day government in rural South India rests on the same view of government, but it has been modified through foreign influence in the direction of increasing centralization, bureaucracy, and concern for the welfare of the individual. Although the villages have benefited from government-directed famine relief, public health, education, and rural development programs, there has been a substantial loss of autonomy. The Village Headman and the Village Accountant, formerly hereditary officers, have become salaried employees of the government with a corresponding loss of authority and the ability to control local events. *Tahsildars*, once the authoritative rulers of minor principalities containing several hundred villages and their regional market town, have also become salaried government officials with sharply curtailed powers. In effect, the rule of dharma has been replaced by the rule of law. The rule of dharma was an authentic local growth which represented tradition—things as they had always been. The rule of law is a hybrid of colonial bureaucracy, British democracy, and Indian dharma.

Because the tissue uniting the village with its government is a mosaic in which the bureaucracy of a modern urban welfare state competes with the elements of a sometimes resurgent traditional form of government, the government is in many ways the least comprehensible part of the village environment. Formally, Gopalpur, Namhalli, and Elephant are linked to the government in more or less the same way (except for recent changes resulting from the introduction of elected village councils). Gopalpur and Namhalli both possess Village Headmen and Accountants, although in both cases the Accountant is not a resident. The Headman is responsible for keeping order and for receiving and assisting visiting government officials of all kinds. The Accountant is primarily responsible for keeping land records. The Headman and Accountant, together with a kind of bailiff, are responsible for the collection of taxes. In Gopalpur, the Village Headman is assisted by a Police Headman who handles routine village business. Elephant is technically a hamlet of a larger village. Its records are kept elsewhere, and there is disagreement concerning the respective duties of the traditional Headman and the representatives of the Headman and Accountant of the larger village. In all three villages, the somewhat different allegiances of the village officials lead to a state of chronic competition and sometimes open conflict among them. This division of leadership is sometimes viewed as an asset by higher government officials who play off one village leader against another to obtain information or cooperation.

Village schoolteachers in Namhalli, and also very recently in Gopalpur and Elephant, are accountable only to their supervisors within the educational establishment. Only in Namhalli, which has had a school since 1903, do the teachers come from the village. No other local government officials are present in any of the three villages. In larger villages these officials might include a Revenue Inspector charged with supervising tax collections, a Village Level Worker concerned with rural development, a police officer, a postman, a midwife, and various forest officials. These officials are usually assigned a number of villages which they are supposed to visit periodically. They tend to visit the larger villages frequently, but are rarely seen in small villages and hamlets.

Other government officials are located in a *Tahsil* headquarters town and form a kind of cabinet to the Tahsildar. In former times, when Tahsil towns were often isolated, the Tahsildar was very nearly as powerful as the local chieftain he replaced. In modern times, with improved communication and greater departmental supervision of the Tahsil officers, the importance of the Tahsildar has steadily declined. Governmental activities have shifted from an almost exclusive emphasis on keeping order and collecting taxes to an increasing involvement in such welfare-oriented programs as education, public health, and agricultural development.

The influence of the government on any particular village depends on such characteristics as its population, size, accessibility, politically influential individuals, and level of education. A large village may contain a considerable staff of minor government officials, while a small village or hamlet may lack even a schoolteacher. Small, poor, and inaccessible, a typical hamlet may have no direct connection with the government, may never have been visited by any but the lowest level of government functionaries, and may be completely dominated by a single influential individual in a nearby large village.

Elephant is, or was until recently, a good example of a small and inaccessible village with poor and illiterate inhabitants. In 1952, its only educational facility was a folk school which operated independently of the government under the supervision of a teacher hired by the parents of the five or six children who attended it 12 hours daily. Instruction consisted of memorization of the traditional epics, the *Ramayana* and the *Mahabharata*. People in the village believed they were still ruled by the British East India Company, a fact of which they seemed inordinately proud.

They were aware of the existence of a Tahsildar located in a distant town and of a District Commissioner who supervised the Tahsildar. They were unaware of any of the mechanics of government or of any techniques for making their grievances known. When the area surrounding the village was made into a reserved forest and the location of the village was changed, they acquiesced without complaint. When elephants began consuming the village crops, they sent an emissary to the Tahsildar, who suggested that any offending elephant be brought to his office. This jocular response to a serious problem can charitably be attributed to the probability that the Tahsildar had been raised in an urban environment and lacked the slightest conception of the problems of the "unimportant" forest villages under his control.

Thus, people in Elephant viewed the Tahsildar as a distant but all-powerful potentate. They were only vaguely aware that a District Commissioner exercised supervision over him. As late as 1966, they were also unaware of the fact that two years earlier they had been assigned to a new district.

The isolation of Elephant and of the villages surrounding it resulted, in traditional times, in the rule of the region by a single individual who might best be described as a bandit chief. The conquest of the region by Citizen Tipu Sultan, an ally of Napoleon who ruled much of South India in the late 1700s, and the conquest of Tipu Sultan by the British were noted by people living in the region but had little effect on their daily life. The sweeping political and social changes of the past century have largely escaped the notice of people in Elephant. Perhaps during the nineteenth century, when government officials were more accustomed to surveying their domains on horseback, Elephant had more regular contact with its government. During the twentieth century, as government officials tended increasingly to be urban and educated bureaucrats, the burden of paperwork and the decline of horsemanship combined to isolate Elephant and its neighboring villages from any direct contact with middle-class government officials.

India, like most of the less industrialized nations, lacks the financial resources and trained personnel required to maintain an "incorruptible" government bureaucracy. Partly as a legacy of colonialism, when only a handful of men at the Tahsil, or administrative town, level—the Tahsildar, the doctor, and the Police Inspector—might have been British, and partly as a result of the absence of trained personnel, the "incorruptible" middle-class backbone of government ends abruptly at the Tahsil headquarters. These government officials are not literally incorruptible, but villagers generally lack the funds required to corrupt them. Lower-ranking government officials, those who come into direct contact with villagers, are generally underpaid, undereducated, undersupervised, and far from home. In mountain regions, where villages are far apart and are rarely visited by middle-class officials likely to be contemptuous of petty graft and corruption, low-ranking government officials sometimes abandon themselves to orgies of graft and corruption.

During the two months in 1952 that I conducted fieldwork in Elephant, minor forest service officials, often in armed gangs, visited Elephant several times each week, levying fines, searching houses, and punishing those who criticized their activities. One of Elephant's village officials describes the situation as follows:

> We are afraid of the king [i.e., the government]. We think he may fine us heavily or imprison us, so we pay whatever the guards demand and build our small houses. If we do any other work in the forest without their permission, they will put up a case against us.
>
> Yesterday they came here and took a week's supply of millet from each house, along with beans and clarified butter. If we don't give what they ask, they go into our houses, remove our firewood, and put up a case against us. We are illiterate, we don't know how to deal with them, we don't know the rules and regulations of the government.
>
> Collectively, if we oppose them, they make a separate case, saying that the people of such and such a village assaulted them.

Until recently, village officials collected taxes without giving receipts, largely under the principle of "from each according to his ability to pay."

Isolated villages like Elephant, which lack literate and powerful citizens, are exposed to a government in which the police powers of the modern state fall into the hands of unscrupulous minor officials who carry on policies of almost limitless exploitation. In former times, when the power of the state was much more restricted and government was more at the level of a tribal chiefdom, Elephant probably enjoyed greater freedom from exploitation, but it still lacked the protections of law and tradition that characterized governmental relationships in larger kingdoms located in more settled regions.

Elephant's adaptation, which can be taken as typical of tribal and isolated village peoples in South India, is essentially one of flight and concealment. Contact with government officials is avoided if possible, usually by hiding in the forest. It is startling and dismaying to enter a village in the Elephant region and find it depopulated except for a few ancients who are too tired and too old to flee to the forest. Only after the old men have been convinced that the visitors are harmless does the rest of the population slowly return to make them welcome.

Wealth is, of course, carefully concealed. Gold is hidden in hollowed-out places in the bamboo rafters that support the thatched roofs of houses. Grain is buried in carefully constructed pits in the village streets. Clothing is cheap and in some cases practically nonexistent. Houses are small and poorly constructed. In 1952, the only evidence of substantial wealth in Elephant was the elaborate construction of stone walls and terraces on agricultural lands. The village was also in the process of constructing a large mathe, a kind of religious institution for entertaining travelers and visitors from neighboring villages. These uses or displays of wealth are nonportable and do not easily reveal the builder's identity.

After 1952, a government investigation of conditions in the Elephant region led to the punishment and transfer of the individuals responsible for pillaging the village. In addition, a post office was constructed in a nearby town and a well-trained government teacher was assigned to the village. The combined presence of a single educated individual and good postal service brought an end to the discontinuity between official government policy and the actual behavior of government officials in the region. The possibility of direct communication between the villagers of Elephant and the "incorruptible" officials in the Tahsil headquarters brought about the almost instantaneous disappearance of the old patterns of exploitation.

Because traditional Elephant was a millet-raising village with relatively low crop yields, it lacked a class of wealthy investors who might have had influence with high-ranking government officials. The rugged nature of the countryside, the low density of population, and the substantial distances between villages created a situation in which local urban centers could not develop and in which stable government could not thrive. The development of stable and consistent relationships with centers of government had to await the growth of a more honest officialdom as well as the education and literacy required for communication with higher levels of authority.

Although modern Gopalpur, like Elephant, preserves a relatively traditional pattern of village-government relationships, the pattern represented in Gopalpur is characteristic of a highly productive agricultural region located close to centers of government power. Gopalpur is less than a hundred miles from the ruins of Hampi, the capital city of the medieval Vijayanagar Empire, and it is surrounded on all sides by the still-thriving cities of the Muslim potentates who brought about the fall of the empire. Although Gopalpur, like Namhalli, lies in a border area between Kannada- and Telugu-speaking regions, its closeness to seats of power has resulted in an alternation of strong governments rather than in an absence of government or domination by distant and therefore ineffective governments.

In 1800, when the British defeated Tipu Sultan, the northern territories of Mysore State, including Gopalpur, were given to the Nizam of Hyderabad, who had allied himself with the British. Although the Nizam gradually introduced a bureaucratic government cast in the colonial mold, the state of Hyderabad remained a traditional government relatively uninfluenced by the "incorruptible" bureaucrats of the Indian Civil Service. Because Hyderabad was not conquered in a military sense, its traditional rural elite survived the British period intact.

In recent years, after a comic-opera war in which the Nizam's largely decorative army fled precipitately from Indian government tanks and troops, the region surrounding Gopalpur was returned to the government of Mysore. The town of Yadgiri, Gopalpur's Tahsil headquarters, with its 118° hot season temperatures, is now regarded as a hardship post, to which officials guilty of corruption or lacking in seniority and political influence may be transferred. Isolated, more than 300 miles from the seat of government, the officials of the "New Mysore" vainly attempt to exert a modernizing influence in a place where they are regarded as oppressive foreigners and agents of a democracy thoroughly repugnant to the powerful aristocracy of the region.

Although a heroic official of the new government sometimes achieves modest gains, the political power of the traditional aristocracy is such that ambitious and incorruptible officials are all too likely to receive the transfers for which they have almost certainly applied. The political power of the aristocracy arises from its possession of vast acreages of fertile black soil and irrigated rice land. The high yield and great value of these lands is the ecological factor that supports, and under traditional arrangements necessitates the development of an investor class in the region. Members of the yeoman class require capital, obtained through loans, to farm their lands.

In effect, the government of the Gopalpur region is in the hands of a powerful aristocratic class capable of exerting absolute control over the lives and fortunes of ordinary villagers. Historically, the application of this power has been restrained by traditionally enforced reciprocal obligations, by competition between aristocrats for supporters, and by the threat of armed rebellion. To a large degree, the power of the landed aristocrat depends on the support he receives from his followers. This support requires the establishment of a traditionally sanctioned patron-client relationship. In this relationship, the client is expected to make regular payments of interest, to furnish field labor at harvesttime, and to provide armed support in the event of conflict. The client depends on his patron for seed at planting time and for loans of grain and cash during times of hardship. To earn cash for their marriages, clients' sons expect employment in the patron's household, and throughout the year the patron is expected to carry out lavish ceremonials at which hundreds or even thousands of people receive free food. The patron is obligated to support his client in the event of village quarrels and to protect his client's person and property from enemies. In the event of conflict among his clients, the patron plays the role of judge and lawgiver.

Although some families in the Gopalpur region have retained political and economic power over long periods of time, most patrons do not represent a hereditary aristocracy. Rural aristocrats can be drawn from any of the large yeoman farmer jatis, ranging from lowly Shepherd or Muslim to exalted Brahman. There is a continuous circulation from yeoman farmer to aristocrat, in which a successful farmer with many sons and supporters may gradually rise to dominate his own and neighboring villages. His rise is viewed with alarm by more established patrons, who may send their clients to rob his house, beat up his followers, or assassinate him. The rising small patron counters by forming alliances with other patrons, often by borrowing money from them. If he is successful, it is the established patron whose clients are lured away, whose house is robbed, and who is accidentally killed by a pair of savage bullocks that just happen to be in the street when he is walking by. A "great house" may also be weakened by family quarrels and resulting divisions of property. As a patron becomes increasingly secure and powerful, and as his estate is taken over by heirs who have been raised by servants obedient to their every wish, his clients are likely to be subjected to increasing oppression. The clients may then consider betraying their traditional patron and giving their allegiance to some other, more generous, patron.

Thus, membership in the rural elite has been based on a kind of merit, involving the ability to maintain fruitful alliances and fulfill traditional obligations to clients. Mean and oppressive patrons soon acquire a region-wide notoriety, and the collapse of their small empires follows. During 1966, in a sample of 30 villages surrounding Gopalpur, one such patron lost most of his wealth in a robbery abetted by some of his own clients; two were murdered; and one was severely gored by a pair of bullocks said to have been specially trained for the task. A patron who had encouraged his followers to stone the Subinspector of Police found his village surrounded by 70 armed policemen who arrested him and his followers.

Although competition between patrons and periodic rebellions result in a constant substitution of one patron for another, the system itself remains intact because the clients require working capital and protection. Great patrons, who control many villages and feed many people, receive the adulation and support accorded to any benevolent monarch. Rebellion, when it occurs, represents a search for an ideal patron and never an attempt to overthrow a system which the liberal outsider might regard as oppressive. As far as the ordinary villager is concerned, any patron is better than none.

Traditionally, the patrons acted as village and regional chieftains who constituted the government, collecting taxes and paying tribute to the representatives of kingdoms and empires. When bureaucratic government was introduced, the patrons remained outside the system but controlled it through their economic and political influence. Government officials who visit villages are expected to come to the houses of powerful patrons, and their ability to carry out their assigned tasks usually depends on the patrons' goodwill. Patrons who wish to be regarded as progressive promote rural electrification, access roads, schools, and even playgrounds. Conservative patrons are stingy in their hospitality to government officials and encourage them to go elsewhere. A few supplement their income by obtaining government contracts for the construction of wells, irrigation works, and roads. Inspectors are bribed to certify the completion of projects which are never finished. Except for a handful of progressive villages, then, government in the Gopalpur region follows the traditional pattern of collecting taxes and keeping order.

Similar patterns of patron-client relationships are common throughout South India, but the presence of conflicting states and kingdoms in the Gopalpur region has created a somewhat untypical pattern of instability and violence. Elsewhere, near the stable centers of major kingdoms, membership in the patron and investor class is more likely to be hereditary. In some places, Tanjore in Madras, for example, the status of patron may become the prerogative of a single jati, such as the Brahmans, and the yeoman may be reduced to the status of tenant farmer. In modernizing regions, in the heartland surrounding Mysore city, for example, the patron may become exceptionally benevolent and progressive.

Insofar as the Gopalpur region is concerned, the system of patron-client relationships represents a kind of stable disorder in which farmers and patrons who maintain and shift their allegiances with sufficient cleverness achieve a substantial measure of protection and support. The system survives as an anachronism within a bureaucratic governmental setting, and it is hard to see how it can adapt to the pressures generated by the development of new schemes of rural credit or the introduction of increasing numbers of relatively incorruptible civil servants. Because relationships between patrons and between patrons and clients involve elements of illegal violence, even minor improvements in law enforcement would strike a devastating blow at the system. The system is adapted to a situation in which unsettled conditions and constantly shifting centers of state power inhibit the development of a stable and centralized government. As the government of Mysore extends its influence in the Gopalpur region, it seems probable that these relationships and the political system they have supported will disappear.

In contrast to Gopalpur, the Namhalli region has always lacked the resources required for the development of a substantial investor class. Within the village, power resided in a council consisting of a representative from each of the major jatis. In traditional Namhalli, the Village Headman distributed lands on an egalitarian basis, giving a plough of land (about five acres) to each able-bodied male. At harvesttime, the Headman collected taxes in the form of a fixed percentage of the harvested grain. Part of this grain was stored in his house—the only substantial house in the village—and used to make loans to the village farmers. In this sense, the Headman was a patron and the villagers were his clients, but he was rarely as omnipotent as the patrons of Gopalpur.

In settled times, a portion of the grain collected in taxes was given to a local chieftain, who used it to support mercenary soldiers or to pay tribute to more powerful chieftains. Historically, such local chieftains appear to have had indifferent success in bringing law and order to their regions. In consequence, each village was an armed camp surrounded by mud walls and thorn hedges. When armed men appeared at the gates, the inhabitants cowered in their houses while the village officials negotiated the amount of tribute to be paid. During the nineteenth century, this system of non-government was gradually replaced by a local bureaucracy which differed only in the smallest details from the government bureaucracy that until recently has proved ineffective in Elephant and Gopalpur. In Namhalli, despite a few transitory difficulties, it was to prove remarkably effective because it did not have to contend with the isolation characteristic of Elephant or the concentrations of power characteristic of Gopalpur.

Since Namhalli was located on the invasion route followed by the British armies during the conquest of Mysore, its first experience with the new British government was less than ideal. In fact, the village appears to have been destroyed at that time. Namhalli was later resettled under a government policy in which lands were auctioned off to whoever would agree to pay the most taxes. By the 1830s, this system of tax collection had proved disastrous, and a British-run bureaucratic government was introduced. Although Mysore city, some 60 miles to the east, remained the official capital of Mysore state, which ostensibly remained an independent native state, the effective capital now became the town of Bangalore, only a few miles from Namhalli. Namhalli was also within an hour's walk of the major roads and railroads leading to Madras.

Because minor government officials in the Namhalli region operated virtually in the shadow of their supervisors in Bangalore, the graft and oppression characteristic of Elephant and Gopalpur received little encouragement. A government primary school was established in Namhalli in 1903, and by World War I educated villagers had a fairly good grasp of the nature of their government and of how to secure favorable treatment from its officials.

Namhalli's proximity to the centers of government resulted in a long list of benefits, especially in terms of individual welfare—famine relief, control of epidemic disease, access to a rapidly developing urban market, education, efficient police services, honest tax collection, and agricultural improvements, including the moldboard plow and a wide variety of new crops. The village social order did not fare quite as well. The old Village Headman lost all his property when harvest gluts following the introduction of cash taxation made it impossible for him to pay land taxes. In 1911, a new Headman was deposed because he couldn't keep his books straight. Government efforts to regularize the village council system resulted in its gradual collapse. Nearness to the city combined with intervals of economic prosperity led to periods of rapid cultural change, during which opposing values and a lack of strong leadership induced conflicts that could not be resolved by the barely functioning village council. Government welfare activities also led to a rapid growth of population. By 1952, the economic gains of 70 years of "good" government had been virtually wiped out, and overpopulation was placing severe pressure on village lands. Internally, the village was in a state of almost total disruption, conflict was endemic, and vital ceremonies could no longer be held.

In sharp contrast to Elephant and Gopalpur, where pre-British relationships to government retain considerable importance, Namhalli's traditional government is essentially the British-influenced colonial system. The remembered history of Namhalli is one of continuous change brought about by well-intentioned government policies. These policies resulted in greater agricultural productivity and increased population. They stimulated the development of an economy based on the increasing use of cash and involvement of the village in urban and international patterns of exchange. All of Namhalli's ecological and social relationships came to be influenced by a pattern of growth characterized by the more or less continuous introduction of new technology and new ideas.

By the early 1950s, the ecological imbalances created by continuous change had resulted in excessive utilization of dry lands to the point where the village could no longer support itself exclusively by agriculture. Change and increasing government regulation had created a situation in which the traditional social organization could no longer function effectively. Thus, by the early 1950s, the potential for adaptation inherent in Namhalli's traditions seems to have been exhausted. Later in the decade, the traditional pattern of an essentially passive reaction to government policies and to change began to give way to more active policies which involved Namhalli in the direct manipulation of government and the exploitation of opportunities for salaried employment in government and in the city. These later changes are discussed in Chapter 10.

From an ecological standpoint, the kinds of relationship with government that were maintained in Elephant and Gopalpur represent a relatively stable situation in which substantial amounts to produce were exchanged (in the form of taxes or interest) for protection or sometimes simply for the privilege of being left alone. In the mythical period before the coming of the British, Namhalli's relationships were almost certainly of the same type. In Elephant and Gopalpur today, and in Namhalli until the 1950s, the general pattern of relationship to government was passive. The villagers gave taxes to the government or interest to patrons and received in return whatever reward or punishment the raja decreed. In each village, the balance of reward and punishment was strongly affected by local environmental conditions. Gopalpur paid for and received a substantial measure of protection in a politically unstable environment. Elephant, due to its isolation, paid much and received very little in return. Namhalli, especially after the introduction of cash taxation, paid smaller and smaller taxes each year as a result of continuing inflation, and received ever-increasing benefits as a result of its proximity to newly established centers of power.

Because South Indian governmental structures have changed more rapidly and more frequently than any other aspect of the village environment, it is difficult to obtain the kind of timeless perspective on relationships to government that we get when we consider relationships to the natural environment. The existence of long-established patterns of intermarriage and economic exchange between villages supports the idea that the peacekeeping and protective functions of government were carried out effectively. In traditional times, warfare could usually be conducted by mercenaries paid with tax monies, so the villager was often sheltered from economic and physical injury while states and empires rose and fell around him. In the modern period, the protective function of government has been carried to its logical extreme. South India has been free of warfare for nearly two centuries.

In this chapter, "government" has been taken to refer to those political agencies charged with collecting taxes, enforcing order, and keeping peace. Although traditional governments occasionally constructed irrigation works, they lacked any strong concern for the regulation of individual conduct, education, public health, arbitration of disputes, or improvement of the circumstances of life. Many of these functions were carried out by religious institutions which existed almost independently of the political state. The religious order counterbalanced the political order and formed a separate and important aspect of the environment of the individual village. The following chapter considers the ecological importance of South Indian religious institutions and rituals.

Chapter 9

RELIGIOUS RITUALS AND INSTITUTIONS

In previous chapters, the concepts of dharma and karma have been shown to play a fundamental role in influencing the specific choices made among the various options avialable for coping with the natural and social environments within which the village functions. Dharma is the key concept of the South Indian world view, and it is a religious concept. Traditional rulers and leaders were responsible for enforcing dharma, but the problem of defining and explaining its nature was the duty of religious leaders and the institutions they controlled.

Although both church and state in traditional India lacked the centralized and bureaucratic organization typical of modern societies, the dividing line between the various statelike and churchlike institutions was sharply drawn. The state and local governments collected taxes and maintained a kind of order, while the church, if it can be called that, regulated birth, marriage, and death, and attended to the many details of day-to-day conduct. But it must be observed from the start that from an organizational standpoint, the religion called Hinduism consists of a variety of conflicting sects and viewpoints and is totally lacking in centralized controls.

South Indian Hinduism derives such order and continuity as it attains by virtue of the fact that all sects base their teachings on scriptural authorities that share the same basic concepts of dharma and karma, although they label and define these and other religious concepts in different ways. Religious sects may sometimes impose distinctive behavior upon their adherents; Lingayats must dine only with each other and practice vegetarianism regardless of their original jati membership. More commonly, the sect, on the basis of karma, reinforces the traditional duties and customs of the different jatis that adhere to it. Especially at the village level, Hinduism derives part of its strength and persistence from the fact that its priests and practitioners tend to reinforce traditional behavior.

Most jatis recognize particular gurus, or religious instructors, who, in conjunction with jati elders, define correct behavior, establish membership in the jati, regulate marriage and ceremonial life, and settle disputes among members. Although gurus are considered to be hierarchically ranked in some kind of organization, especially within the Lingayat jati, the authority of a guru over his followers or of a high-ranking over a low-ranking guru is almost entirely moral. The official gurus of jatis generally hold their positions through inheritance or appointment by their predecessors.

To the ordinary villager in Gopalpur, Namhalli, or Elephant, all temples and holy places, including Hindu and Muslim holy places, are sacred. Worship at all of them is appropriate, and, should his jati guru prove unavailable, he can seek the advice of any religious man in connection with the settlement of disputes about proper behavior. Details of birth, marriage, and funeral ceremonies are determined by village priests, usually Brahmans or members of the Lingayat priestly jati. Priesthoods of villages, jatis, or lineages are usually hereditary. Each village temple also possesses its own hereditary priest.

In the event of major crises, or simply to gain merit, individuals make pilgrimages to lineage or jati religious centers or to other places as close as the next village or as far away as Banaras, a famous pilgrimage center in North India. If a village or the members of one of its jatis wish to do so, they may also invite important gurus to visit for the purposes of settling quarrels or giving their blessings. Because important gurus travel on elephants and with large retinues, such visits may be quite expensive.

Because the development of a major pilgrimage center is based on the spiritual power of its location and deity, a fact attested by the millions of people who have been cured of chronic illness or have overcome infertility as a result of pilgrimages to it, the guru of such a place is an international figure with powers and resources quite independent of any local raja. The development of pilgrimage centers and of lineage, jati, and sectarian gurus, often with millions of followers, creates a counterforce to the secular power of the state. The wise raja conforms to dharma, as defined by his guru, in the collection of taxes and the administration of his kingdom.

Historically, the Muslim rulers, Tipu Sultan of Mysore and the Nizam of Hyderabad, worshiped at Hindu shrines adjoining their palaces. The collapse of the Moghul Empire in North India is attributed to Aurangzeb's support of Islam and his consequent failure to maintain the allegiance of his Hindu subjects. A traditional ruler might well undertake to settle disputes between jatis or to enforce rules about appropriate dress and conduct. When he interfered with traditional prerogatives about such things as taxation or compensation for the performance of jati duties, he did so at his peril, for now he was not enforcing dharma but committing adharma. Punitive boycotts and open rebellion were the likely result of such conduct. Control of the raja by means of religious appeals is still politically important. The Telugu linguistic state of Andhra was created a few years ago only after a political leader demonstrated his sincerity by the religious technique of fasting unto death, and it was Gandhi's religious appeal, signified by the title Mahatma, or great soul, which led to Indian independence.

Although political and religious institutions can be regarded as counterbalancing forces in their impact on village life, direct opposition between political and religious figures does not appear to have been common. At both local and state levels, political officials generally conducted their tax collections and military operations within the limits defined by religion. Ceremonies legitimating succession to office and marriage could not be conducted in the event of direct opposition between political and religious institutions. Traditionally, tax collection itself involved worship of the heap of harvested grain and its consequent division among priests, tax collectors, and occupational specialists providing services to the farmer. Although some political figures may have wished for a larger portion of the harvested grain than that decreed by dharma, there is an obvious advantage to rituals that make the payment of taxes a religious obligation.

Enlightened self-interest and good public relations may have been sufficient to ensure the good conduct of the raja and other political figures, but the power of dharma and karma, inherent in the South Indian world view, was probably the major factor influencing the conduct of government. When dharma was present and individuals and jatis were obedient to their karma and performed their duties accordingly, the village and the kingdom prospered. When dharma was absent, famine, epidemic, and military disaster were the inevitable punishments. Because the raja was specifically responsible for enforcing dharma, he was personally responsible for disasters. Although a few traditional rulers may have manipulated these notions in a cynical and unbelieving way, most accepted and believed in them.

The dissemination of basic religious and world-view concepts at all levels of society was the primary function of the guru, or religious preceptor. Gurus were often associated with important temples or religious centers, but they might also be ordinary men or women who established their religiosity by adopting an ascetic life-style. Each jati, including the kingly jatis, had official and often hereditary gurus who maintained genealogical records by means of which the individual could validate his membership and who always served as a resort in times of crisis. All problems, from crop failure to marital quarrels, were problems of dharma, and all could be resolved through consultation with gurus whose familiarity with the scriptures or direct and saintly religious experience guaranteed their knowledge of proper behavior. Although an official jati guru might be a distant and unknown figure, other educated and saintly individuals were always available.

One guru, located at a major shrine not far from Gopalpur, published a hymnbook in the regional dialect. Few individuals can actually read and follow such a hymnal, but the hymns were soon memorized and sung at sessions held almost nightly during slack seasons in most of the villages of the region. There are also various kinds of professional singers and storytellers who provide the most illiterate of villagers with a fund of detailed religious knowledge. Giving grain or cash to such religious mendicants is an efficacious way of compensating for sins the individual may have committed.

In general, people in Gopalpur lack any direct contact with gurus associated with major religious shrines. Very often the role

of personal guru is taken over by the patron, who is usually educated and therefore knowledgeable concerning dharma. A religious
ascetic living in a nearby abandoned temple is consulted by a few,
but many feel that he became a recluse only to escape his nagging
wife and that he therefore lacks genuine saintliness. Should the
advice given by local patrons and educated men prove ineffective,
resort can be had to a genuine saint, a woman living in a temple
some ten miles distant who is said to subsist on air and water.

In both Namhalli and Elephant, the role of gurus and religious
figures in adjudicating disputes and teaching dharma is more
powerful than in Gopalpur. In Namhalli, older men typically retire
to their gardens when their children begin to take over household
responsibilities. Because the gardens must be guarded constantly
from animals and humans, the old man living in his garden house
performs a useful economic function. At the same time, he achieves
the isolation required for meditation and religious devotion. Such
old men may seek personal gurus to assist them in their medita-
tions, and they may themselves acquire followers who accept their
teachings concerning dharma. Although government schools and
other modernizing influences are often thought to have a weak-
ening effect on religious ideologies, since the founding of Namhalli's school, in 1903, its teachers have been deeply religious men
whose instruction emphasized dharma as well as arithmetic.

Until recently, jati gurus and other major religious figures visited
Namhalli frequently. In 1952, the Village Headman brought in a
minor guru of the Lingayat sect to conduct a fire-walking ceremony
at which members of the Lingayat and Lingayat Priest jatis demonstrated their religious purity by walking over burning coals.
Earlier, during the 1930s, the village was visited by a guru of the
low-ranking Adikarnatica, or Leatherworker jati, who assigned to
representatives of the higher-ranking Blacksmith and Oil Merchant jatis the duty of serving as gurus to the local Adikarnatica.
While present in the village, the guru settled all outstanding disputes, receiving earnest money from both parties and then deduct-
ing suitable fines before returning it. After his departure, the
representatives of the Blacksmith and Oil Merchant jatis were
empowered as gurus to supervise marital ararngements among the
Adikarnatica and also to convene council meetings at which disputes within that jati could be adjudicated. These powers related

not only to the Adikarnatica in Namhalli, but to those in surrounding villages as well.

In view of Elephant's comparative isolation, it might be predicted that fewer connections with outside religious institutions and influences would be present than in the other two villages. Elephant does have relatively few informal sources of religious influence, such as hymn singing or frequent visits by bards and storytellers, but its mathe and village priest provide a far stronger and more direct link with formally organized religious institutions than is possessed by most other villages. Located on the banks of the sacred Cauvery River, the Elephant region derives religious importance from its proximity to that stream. Several hundred years ago, the wildness and sacredness of the region appear to have inspired the building of a series of mathes, or religious pilgrimage centers. These mathes form part of a complex hierarchy of Lingayat shrines stretching, in theory at least, from such international holy places as Mount Everest and Banaras down to smaller regional and local holy places such as Elephant. The entire population of Elephant and much of the population of its region consists of members of the priestly Lingayat jati who came to settle in the vicinity of the mathes.

Unlike the ordinary temple priest, whose principal duties consist of receiving offerings, the Svamiji attached to a mathe undertakes the duties of a Catholic parish priest. He officiates at all ceremonies and joins village officials in planning improvements, arranging marriages, and settling disputes. In Elephant, the Svamiji is at least theoretically celibate. This gives him great moral authority, and he is unquestionably the most powerful individual in the village. Elephant is a theocracy within which dharma is strictly enforced and rigidly adhered to. Although well-known animosities exist between the Svamiji and some of the village officials and between particular families in the village, disputes are quickly arbitrated at the equivalent of town meetings presided over by the Svamiji. Theft is unknown, and there has been no violent conflict in the community in living memory. Lacking in traditional times any firm connection to a political entity larger than the 20-odd villages located in its tiny valley, the Elephant region was firmly integrated into the larger South Indian civilization by means of its mathes and svamijis. Elephant is an extreme demonstration of the observation that ancient Indian civilization was culturally rather than politically or socially integrated.

Formal religious institutions such as jati gurus or the hierarchy of Lingayat mathes may sometimes, as in Elephant, exert direct influence on the lives of ordinary villagers. More often, the religious teachings of active saints and gurus spread indirectly through literate priests, village storytellers and bards, and religious seekers, such as the retired elders of Namhalli. In the South Indian village it is impossible to hear a song, attend a play, or listen to a story without receiving information about dharma and karma, the rights and obligations that individuals have toward each other. It is impossible to overestimate either the role of this shared religious tradition in facilitating social interaction within the village and between villagers and outsiders or the importance of religious figures in the arbitration of disputes.

Religious institutions also disseminate information about the proper conduct of ritual activities. Rituals conducted at the local level may be scaled-down versions of those conducted at major shrines and temples. Alternatively, they may be taken directly from scriptural sources or based on instructions provided by a guru. The accepted purpose of ritual activities is to make offerings to deities in exchange for supernatural support of human activities. Properly conducted *pujas*, or rituals, may have a compelling effect on deities, but most villagers are skeptical that their rituals are scrupulous or elegant enough to have such effects. Basically, the village ritual is an appeal or prayer for support. It is also a means of cleansing the village and the individual. It provides a framework for the performance of good deeds. In effect, the good deeds performed in ritual provide the means of balancing the supernatural books, which often carry a large deficit of bad deeds committed in the course of everyday life.

In this context, crop failure, disease, and other misfortunes are regarded as supernatural punishments sent to afflict those who have been weighed in the balance and found to have accumulated more bad deeds (karma) than good deeds (dharma). Here, dharma and karma are used in a restricted sense. In Namhalli in 1952, when rains were late and scanty, a standard reply to questions about the weather was, "Sin is up, we will get no rain." Although charity and other good deeds may help to compensate for such a situation, the only really effective answer is especially zealous performance of community rituals or, in extremity, the performance of special rituals.

Because drought and epidemics endanger the entire community, rituals designed to prevent or halt such disasters must involve all its members. Because all are affected, the sins of all must be removed or counterbalanced. Rituals at the individual, family, community, or regional level restore dharma and thus guarantee the proper functioning of all things. The performance of ritual is therefore viewed as the single most important means of regularizing and maintaining ecological relationships between the community and the world around it.

Since full participation is in some measure an act of voluntary goodwill, the *sine qua non* of a successful ritual performance is a kind of universal goodwill closely resembling our "Christmas spirit." Any ritual can be "spoiled" by angry words or refusal to participate, and almost any ritual can be used as a forum for the adjudication of conflict. Typically, when called upon to participate, the aggrieved individual refuses to perform his scripturally assigned task or refuses to accept his assigned share of the offering that has been made. The ritual then comes to a halt until the Big Men, who are always present at important rituals, arrange a settlement of the grievance. In other cases, serious conflicts are suspended during the ritual days. In Gopalpur, the need for peace in ritual was so great that sworn enemies, men who had killed each other's fathers and brothers, would cooperate with every appearance of amity. Although there was no question that the enemies were merely waiting for an opportunity to break each other's heads, the ritual forced them to exhibit peaceful behavior. Once having demonstrated amity, both parties might be reluctant to be the first to commit a subsequent breach.

Ritual also has important effects in regulating relationships between villages. This is most clearly demonstrated in the Gopalpur region, where the four months of the hot season are taken up with elaborate intervillage festivals, performances conducted by one village to which guests from other villages are invited. With few exceptions, these festivals are celebrated by villages with a previous history of internal conflict between opposed parties. A festival can be held only if each household contributes cash and cooperation, and its annual performance requires the cooperation of the opposed parties. The most likely explanation for the high cor-

156 / VILLAGE LIFE IN SOUTH INDIA

relation between internal conflict and holding festivals is that the
celebration brightens the reputation of a village that is known to
be the scene of disputes. Disaster will surely follow if a festival is
not performed regularly and this also may serve to keep conflict
within bounds. Furthermore, the weeks of preparation required
for the festival occupy a time of year when heat and idleness are
most likely to trigger disputes.

Because the festivals would be pointless if the guests failed to
show up, their performance requires a comparative absence of
intervillage conflict and enmity. These performances can also be
interpreted as a form of competition for prestige, and it can be
argued that such legitimated competition between villages tends
to suppress the illegitimate conflicts that might otherwise interfere
with marital relationships or trade.

In the Gopalpur region, intervillage competition is also expressed
in wrestling matches that are held at the time of festivals. Although
the activity itself is a relatively mild form of hand wrestling involving teams from different villages, it often results in violent riots
that may lead to loss of life. Some years ago, during the 1960s,
seven people were reported killed in such a riot at a village near
Gopalpur. Although wrestling matches are a less than ideal way
of preventing conflict, they do serve to occupy much of the free
time of young men between the ages of 15 and 30 and help to
replace warfare as an expression of hostility between villages.
Furthermore, even if wrestling riots were as deadly as intervillage
warfare might be, the matches restrict conflict to a particular time
and place where it can usually be controlled by policemen and
village officials. Although violence is more frequent in the Gopalpur region than in Elephant or Namhalli, its disruptive effects are
blunted to a considerable degree by the conflict-resolving and
-regulating mechanisms inherent in ritual.

In the Namhalli region, where intravillage conflict is frequent
but much less violent and intervillage conflict is unheard of, festivals are less dramatic and less time-consuming. Competition between villages takes the form of volleyball matches, which sometimes lead to acrimony but rarely to violence. Although rituals still
serve as a forum for settling disputes, the suppression of violent
conflict is left largely to the police. The presence of relatively
efficient government services has thus had some effect in reducing
the importance of ritual as a means of encouraging cooperation

and reducing the incidence of conflict. In Namhalli, marriage ceremonies have been progressively reduced in importance and may
now be completed in one day instead of seven, and festivals are
held in only a few major villages and towns.

In the Elephant region, rituals are important and frequent but
seem to have little to do with the regulation of conflict, most of
which is adjudicated directly by the Svamiji. The small size of the
villages in the Elephant region and the great distances between
them probably account for the virtual absence of violent conflict.
Religious occasions such as marriage ceremonies and the performance of village dramas serve as major vehicles for intervillage
relationships and can be regarded as critical in maintaining the
region as a single homogeneous unit.

Rituals are necessary activities, but they may be avoided or
postponed during years of low agricultural production. The financial preparations for rituals can therefore be viewed as serving
something like banking purposes. The individual farmer is moti-
vated to produce grain and other products beyond his needs for
immediate consumption in order to participate in ritual activity,
such as the marriage of a son or daughter. Should crops fail, the
wedding can be postponed and the household can survive on its
accumulated grain and cash resources.

For poor people, especially in the Gopalpur region, rituals supply
free meals of meat and rice, especially during the hot season when
there is no work and no other source of income. From February
to June, weddings and festivals take place almost every night and
most of them involve the distribution of free food. The ritual feeding of all comers is much less common in the Namhalli and Elephant regions, where great accumulations of wealth are rare, but
it is nevertheless frequent enough to be of substantial economic
and nutritional significance. A similar motivation, the desire to
accumulate good deeds, or dharma, causes people in Namhalli to
give double handfuls of grain throughout the year to all who come
to the door and ask for it. In Elephant, until 1952, it was considered
sinful to sell milk, which was given freely to all persons passing
through the village.

Charity, whether made available at rituals or at the housedoor,
serves economic as well as religious purposes. The fact that free
food is generally available means that it is unnecessary to pay
agricultural laborers a living wage. It also means that in periods

of local famine it is possible for large populations to survive by wandering to areas with a food surplus. In 1952, regions to the east were more deeply affected by drought than the Namhalli region. For several months, starving people from those regions passed through Namhalli and were given small amounts of grain. When local food supplies began to be depleted, the village adjoining Namhalli passed an ordinance forbidding begging, but Namhalli never did. Charity mitigates the effects of seasonal unemployment and short-run disasters. Long-term overpopulation and hard times have a tendency to dry up the sources of charity, and it is then that people starve.

Ritual dietary taboos divide the South Indian population (including persons of European origin and Muslims) into three roughly equal groups—milk drinkers, mutton eaters, and beef eaters. The largest supplies of beef become available in bad years when cattle begin to die of hunger and disease. Such animals fall by hereditary right into the hands of the lowest-ranking landless laborer jatis—and here again the social and religious systems coincide to support the neediest among the population.

In the Namhalli region, because the irrigation tank in the neighboring town was once saved from destruction by a member of the low-ranking Leatherworker jati, the Leatherworkers had the privilege and obligation of performing an annual ritual in honor of the water goddess, Gangamma (Mother Ganges). Until this ceremony was banned by a government sensitive to the feelings of European meat eaters, up to 100 male water buffalo were slaughtered each year. Female water buffalo are useful producers of creamy milk, but the male buffalo is not considered useful in the Namhalli region and is not protected by the taboos that apply against the slaughter of bullocks.

Religious institutions and rituals possess the same general form in all three regions, but there are important differences in emphasis. In the Gopalpur region, the presence of a class of wealthy patrons tends to reduce the importance of gurus in the resolution of disputes and the management of daily life. In the Elephant region, by contrast, the weakness of political controls is compensated for by the strong local influence of the guru or svamiji. In vegetarian Elephant, animal sacrifice is unknown; in the Gopalpur and Namhalli regions, it is frequent enough to be of nutritional importance. In the Gopalpur region, feeding people on ritual occasions is sufficiently important to be regarded as a prop for the entire system of patron-client relationships and as a major means of supporting the landless laborer class. In Namhalli, the same effect is secured by the custom of providing charity to all who come to the door. In Elephant, where rituals are as important as they are in Gopalpur, their functions are less directly economic and seem to have more to do with providing a framework for the exchange of visits between villages. In the relatively violent setting of the Gopalpur region, festivals play an important role in the regulation of conflict, a role they do not play in Namhalli or Elephant.

All of this suggests that the function of religious institutions and rituals in South India is not so much to regulate the eco-system directly as to provide a flexible set of options that can compensate for problems arising in the operation of regional ecological and social systems. Religion brakes the boistrous competition inherent in Gopalpur's system of patron-client relationships, but in the Elephant region, where the political system is weak, it provides a context for regional unity and village relationships that would otherwise be absent. Problems of social inequality can be solved, as they are in Elephant, by an absence of social and economic distractions. Problems of food distribution can be solved, as they are in Namhalli, by means of charity and government assistance. Problems of political conflict can be solved, again as in Namhalli, by the use of police power. When such problems cannot be solved by economic or political means, they seem to be solved by recourse to the abundance of religious devices made available by that amorphous and unorganized religion known as Hinduism.

Chapter 10

MODERNIZATION: THE NEW ECOLOGY

So far, the ecology of the South Indian village has been discussed in terms of a variety of relatively fixed relationships between the community and its environment. To the extent that communities earn their living through traditional techniques of agricultural production and marketing, change in the overall pattern of relationship between the village and the world around it has been slow. The use of traditional technology precludes any rapid increases in production and sales, and most villages have lacked the wherewithal to embark on programs of rapid technological or social change.

People living in rural communities regard their ways of life and their economies as relatively stable ("It is coming from time immemorial") and deduce from this general orientation that there are only so many goods in this world and that they are not likely to be substantially increased in number or variety. This is the perspective that George Foster has labeled "the principle of limited good." Most Indian farmers, being reasonable and confronted by a relatively unchanging world, base a considerable part of their behavior on such a notion.

For many Indian villagers, traditional patterns of stability and traditional limitations upon the availability of goods have gradually relaxed. As India has developed large and industrialized cities and as new techniques of food production have been introduced, the availability of goods has increased. Transportation and access to markets have improved; agricultural production, though not necessarily food production, has increased over the years, and there are more kinds of things farmers can buy. One response to these changing circumstances has been a dramatic increase in population, made possible by new food crops, improved medical care, and better distribution of food.

India's traditional nonindustrial cities had little to offer in exchange for the agricultural goods they obtained from the farmer. The urban center extracted goods from the countryside through loans at high interest, taxation, the provision of protection from enemies, and assistance in dealing with supernatural powers. The traditional farmer could increase his production through substantial investment in irrigation and land improvement, but the possibility of making such improvements was limited and does not seem to have led to what has been called a "growth economy." To the extent that an individual's status and income were fixed within a relatively stable social and economic hierarchy, there were few strong incentives to increase production or develop new techniques.

The Indian farmer's conservative approach to innovation appears to have been reasonable and pragmatic. He was neither fatalistic nor resistant to change, and he strove to improve his competitive advantage over other farmers by extending his control over land, cattle, and labor. But except where the population had been decimated by famine, epidemic, or war, each farmer's advance involved taking something away from someone else, usually through active political efforts. In traditional times as now, the Indian farmer pursued his own advantage.

Confronted with the changes created by the emergence of government bureaucracy and the modern city, the farmer discovers ways of increasing his economic strength and level of living that do not depend on taking anything away from anybody else. He can export one or two of his male children to the urban job market; he can increase production by importing new techniques or crops; and he can sell his output more conveniently and at a greater profit by using modern means of transportation. Modernization thus offers the farmer a new set of options in an expanding economy, which offer access to what seem to him to be unlimited goods.

The traditional farm community was related to the traditional city in relatively few ways, and the opportunities for profit were limited by traditional restrictions. The modern city offers all the options that were available in the traditional city plus a host of new occupations and new ways of increasing income. Perhaps even more than the traditional city, the modern city exerts its influence unequally over the countryside and consequently offers different sets of opportunities and perspectives to different villages. Looking out from his small community on the myriad complexities and the enormous wealth of the modern city, the farmer now wonders whether he can get a piece of the action.

In the old economy, the farmer profited by obtaining land, bullocks, and hardworking sons. There is no such simple and direct way to exploit the new economy. The city has multiple and complicated needs for manpower and for agricultural goods. To the extent that these needs have already been filled by people coming from other villages and even from other parts of the country, the farmer who is contemplating participation in the modern economy may find no place to go, and his entry into the urban marketplace will be accordingly delayed. Elephant, Gopalpur, and Namhalli have each adapted to the city at different rates and in different ways.

Elephant. In 1952, Elephant was effectively isolated from the modern world by poverty and lack of transportation. The hilly terrain surrounding the village does not permit the use of carts, let alone trucks or buses. A motor road, permitting the establishment of bus and truck transportation, did not reach the nearby town of Tamarind until 1952. Many of the agricultural lands used by Elephant were located in the reserved forest and were subject to constant threats of confiscation. The village had no adequate source of drinking water and a high infant mortality. Under the leadership of its Lingayat priest, the village dedicated a substantial portion of its resources to the construction of a large religious establishment designed to attract pilgrims and thus provide a source of revenue. Funds that might have been used for food, clothing, and housing were dedicated to unsuccessful well-digging projects and the construction of stone terraces intended to increase agricultural production. The village had a small traditional school where children memorized the *Mahabharata* and the *Ramayana;* other community funds contributed only to the welfare of rapacious forest officials.

Houses were tiny, with just enough floor space to accommodate the sleeping family. Most men could not afford the cash or the risk involved in wearing shirts with sleeves or short trousers; conspicuous display of wealth would expose them to officials eager for bribes. Without money, marriages were difficult to arrange and, except for close relatives, people in neighboring villages were reluctant to send their daughters to Elephant. Only the Lingayat priest and a few elders had been to the city, and these men had somehow lost the 500 rupees they took with them to buy furnishings for the village temple. In 1952, there seemed to be no way in which Elephant could modernize.

By 1966, the situation had changed dramatically as a result of the inauguration of an early morning bus service to Bangalore. Milk and clarified butter could be loaded on the bus shortly after dawn and transported to the city in time for late morning delivery. The reserved forest provided Elephant with an abundant source of fodder for cattle, and the sale of milk provided a source of cash. In 1966, the long-planned ceremonial center had been completed. Many more fields had been terraced, and excellent wells for drinking water and for bathing had been completed. Houses had been improved and roofed with machine-made tiles. Improved fields and abundant cow manure had led to a substantial increase in agricultural production. A special house had been constructed for a government school teacher. Through immigration, the importation of daughters' husbands as well as sons' wives, and a tidal wave of children, village population had dramatically increased to meet the increased labor requirements of the new industry.

Although the dramatic increase in Elephant's population was partly a response to increased economic opportunity, it was also a result of improved medical care and, probably, the great importance of child labor in caring for cattle. In view of its rapidly increasing population, Elephant's adaptation to the city cannot be considered stable. While the village can support and employ many children, it cannot support very many additional adults. Further, Elephant's style of adaptation to the urban environment brought in no new skills or special knowledge. Except for the establishment of a government school, Elephant remained a traditional village. Urban influence intensified existing patterns without creating any marked change in the structure of village life.

Because a primary school education opens no doors in the big city, Elephant has no good prospect for maintaining its newfound level of living. Probably Elephant's ultimate adjustment to the city will be in terms of providing unskilled labor. Such an adjustment depends on making a successful entry into a labor market that is neither free nor anonymous. Because employers in Bangalore hire people they know, getting a job involves making contacts and knowing whom to pay off. Up to 1966, Elephant had not successfully placed any of its surplus population in urban jobs.

Gopalpur. Like Elephant, Gopalpur is far from the nearest city and its population is largely uneducated. The nearest city, Hyderabad, is 100 miles to the east; it has developed slowly and offers few opportunities to persons from distant villages. Epidemic diseases and other forms of illness still restrict population growth in the Gopalpur region as do traditional restrictions on marriage and an established pattern of neglecting female children. Direct urban and modernizing influences upon the region have mainly affected wealthy landowners and patrons who have spent large sums on the education of their children and on participation in the urban economy. These men of wealth have tended to become absentee landlords, neglecting traditional social responsibilities and ultimately deserting their villages and giving over their rapidly deteriorating land to tenant farmers who fail to manure them adequately. Other landowners have become aware of modern agricultural techniques, and through mortgage foreclosures and the use of brute force, they have increased the acreages of land under their control in order to make use of tractors and other laborsaving devices.

In general, the wealthy patrons of Gopalpur, anxious to enter the urban middle class, have employed a variety of devices to increase their share of the region's wealth. Rice and sorghum, the principal crops, have been subjected to price control and sometimes forced sale to the government. The inaccessibility of urban markets and the existence of price control have prevented the kinds of adjustment characteristic of such villages as Elephant, and there appear to be no agricultural techniques likely to permit the advantageous exploitation of the urban economy.

During the late 1950s and early 1960s, young men from Gopalpur and other villages, in search of adventure or desperately in need of funds required for marriage and for investment in land

and cattle, began to seek new sources of employment in distant places. Very often, these emissaries to the urban world simply disappeared, never to return.

In my house, there are no economic problems. I told my fourth child not to go to Bombay because there was plenty of work in the house, more than enough work. There were sheep to graze, fields to be plowed, cattle to feed. There was a lot of work.

"I have three older brothers," he said, and he didn't listen to my words. "A lot of people are going to Bombay," he said. "I will go and see it and then come back."

A year later, in 1957, people came to us and said that our son had died in Bombay. I and my husband went there and saw all the companies and mills, but we didn't find out anything. We learned that he had gone to Surat. We went there and asked at all the companies, but we didn't find out anything. We couldn't find our son.

In the house, our son's wife was very sad. She stayed in the house. She didn't have any children. In the house, all of us, all of the older and younger brothers and all of the older and younger sisters, were very sad. We lay in an ocean of sorrow. We heard nothing from our son. We haven't found him anywhere, and no news comes from anywhere. He went to Bombay and he didn't come back.

By 1960, people from Gopalpur had begun to develop the techniques required for survival in Bombay. Stone quarries just outside Bombay were developed by patrons from northern Mysore, and contacts with these men opened up the first few jobs in the big city. By 1966, people from Gopalpur had acquired access to and virtual control over job opportunities in three adjacent stone quarries. Barely literate and totally ignorant of city ways, workers from Gopalpur did not demand large salaries or complain about the company's failure to provide legally required gloves, boots, and safety helmets. The quarries were surrounded by trees and green grass, so even though the people lived in small huts, conditions were relatively healthful. Lacking even the influence required to obtain a ration card, people working in the quarries were often undernourished and covered with bruises and cuts from the quarried rock. But they were earning four times the wages they would have received in Gopalpur.

For the fortunate few who found permanent jobs with companies located inside the city, the pay was much better, but living conditions were unspeakable. People from Gopalpur lived in housing constructed from packing crates and waste lumber containing room for a bed, a cookstove, and nothing more. Communities were established, more or less illegally, on mud flats and other temporarily unused land. For this reason, urban authorities refused to provide water, sewerage, police protection, food rations, and other services. Those who came to Bombay lived in a stinking, fetid swamp surrounded by a mire of feces and garbage fully a foot deep.

Life in the slums of Bombay is organized by bootleggers and gangsters. It is these men who have the influence required to obtain essential ration cards, housing, and factory jobs. One young man from Gopalpur has become a wealthy and successful bootlegger. For the most part, people from Gopalpur come to Bombay in order to earn enough money to pay off outstanding debts and return to the village.

My son went to Bombay because we are poor people and there was poverty in our house. My husband and I had one daughter and one son. After they were born, my husband died and the children were forced to work as laborers. When the children grew up, we arranged for the marriage of my daughter, but there was no money for my son's marriage. For that reason, I went to a wealthy man, got a loan of 600 rupees, and held the marriage. After the marriage, my son stayed in the house for a year, but then the wealthy man sent a man to the house to collect the 600 rupees.

I said to my son, "Go to Bombay, work there, and bring some rupees to pay off our debt." My son's wife went with him to Bombay. At first they worked in the stone quarries, but later my son got a job in a textile mill. He worked and collected 1,000 rupees which he gave to the wealthy man.

Then he went to Bombay again and worked day and night to earn money. He brought 2,500 rupees and purchased a field of dry land. He went back to Bombay and earned enough money to buy some wet land. By 1965, we had ten acres of land.

Each year, he comes back for the village festival and stays here for a month worshiping the gods. Then he goes back to Bombay. This last time he left his wife and child here in the village.

High interest rates and the high price of land force the Bombay worker to return again and again. He goes first as a single man to earn money for his bride-price. He and his wife go to earn money to purchase agricultural land. When the wife has children, she returns to the village, and later the husband returns and the family takes up agriculture again. The money earned in Bombay disappears, into the pocket of the wealthy moneylender or into marginally profitable agriculture. Gopalpur's agricultural economy is supported to some extent by the importation of large amounts of cash from Bombay. Those who go to Bombay spend the better part of their lifetime to achieve the position of middle-class small farmers. Many are unsuccessful in accumulating the necessary cash; others contract tuberculosis and other chronic illnesses and return to the village to die.

Namhalli. Because Namhalli is located only a few miles from Bangalore, it has a long history of relationships with the city. The recent and short-term adaptations to urbanization of such villages as Elephant and Gopalpur seem unsatisfactorily tentative or even destructive, but the longer-term pattern characteristic of Namhalli offers the hope that relationships with the city may ultimately lead to more secure and more satisfactory adaptations. The modernization of Namhalli has resulted from the interaction of six not always highly correlated factors: (1) continued expansion of the authority of the state government at the expense of local and traditional systems of authority; (2) expansion and improvement of systems of transportation, communication, and trade; (3) development of urban manufacturing, trading, and political centers; (4) diffusion of modern bureaucratic systems of education, public health, and welfare; (5) rapid increase of population; and (6) increasing emphasis on a cash economy. The population of Namhalli did not rise consistently with the increase in the first four factors, population having been reduced markedly by the famine of 1876–78 and the influenza epidemic of 1918–19. The availability of cash in Namhalli also fluctuated, increasing rapidly during World Wars I and II and decreasing sharply during the economic depression of the 1930s.

Namhalli's first strong exposure to urban influences occurred during the famine of 1876–78, when the government opened up a soup kitchen near the village. To counteract the effects of the famine, the government distributed cattle and food and constructed irrigation works and railroads. In 1903, a grammar school was constructed in the village, but apart from the now modestly increasing educational level of the population, the years from 1900 to 1914 were relatively stable. Village population grew slowly, land was abundant, and poor market conditions made it difficult to sell agricultural produce. The village lacked sufficient cash to permit any widespread involvement in the urban economy. There was, however, a sharp diminution in the importance of the Village Headman, leadership becoming increasingly diffuse. During this period, the police played a growing role in dealing with serious crime, but for most purposes the village elders were able to maintain their authority through the payment of bribes.

In 1914, with the coming of World War I, the chronic shortage of cash that had restricted participation in the urban economy was alleviated. The price of millet increased fourfold, wages tripled, and the price of land doubled. The public school system and other government services were considerably expanded. Cash earnings were used to purchase machine-made cloth and other urban products. With cash in hand, villagers made increasing use of urban law courts to facilitate the division of property held by large joint families and in some cases to permit the inheritance of property by women. This led to the dissolution of many of the large families, and a steady diminution in family size began. Smaller family size in turn gave greater freedom of action to the heads of nuclear families and made the authority structure of the village progressively less monolithic. Where once the village was dominated by the heads of six large families, by 1953 it was governed by the heads of over 100 small families.

The population of the village increased from 300 in 1881 to 413 in 1901 and 615 in 1953. The increase stimulated more intensive use of the land. Pasture was put under the plow, the number of cattle in the village decreased, and so did the amount of fertilizer available per acre. After 1930, the loss of productivity of the land used to raise millet was counteracted to some extent by the use of new kinds of fertilizer in the rice lands. Even vegetarians did not hesitate to use bone meal on their crops.

Urban involvement also affected the relative economic position of different jatis in the village. Handloom weavers, for example, were put out of business by competition from mill-made cloth. Later, electric looms and government support of the handloom industry made it possible for a few weavers to recover their losses, but the majority were reduced to the status of landless laborers. Moldboard plows introduced by American missionaries in the 1920s and more elaborate carts with iron-rimmed wheels provided increasing employment for members of the Blacksmith jati.

By 1953, Namhalli had more than 30 qualified schoolteachers. Of these, about 12 were employed as teachers, 4 held other kinds of government jobs, and 14 were unemployed. Excluding emigrants and village officials, in 1953 about one person in every six families was employed in a governmental job. With the development of extensive market gardening during World War II, about 75 percent of the families in Namhalli had some sort of access to urban wealth and occupied a rural middle-class of yeoman farmer status.

World War II triggered a pattern of rapid population growth. By 1953, the prosperity brought about by the war had slackened considerably and the village stood roughly at the level reached by Elephant in 1966. Namhalli by 1953 had a large population of young people who were unable to find employment either in agriculture or in urban occupations. Between 1950 and 1955, as population pressure increased and access to urban jobs and markets became increasingly difficult, individual family heads came into increasingly sharp competition over the scarce resources available. The old morality, supported by the domination of a handful of prestigious village elders, disintegrated, but the new urban morality failed to gain the support of urban success. As villagers quarreled over moral and economic issues, with each family attempting to acquire the lands and riches required to provide for growing children, the village became enveloped in chronic conflict. Ceremonies ceased to be held, and temples and irrigation works could not be repaired. There seemed to be no mechanism available to restore consensus or to organize a united attack on the outstanding problems of the village. Addicted to modernization by the economic prosperity following World War II, but now cut off from access to the urban economy, the village suffered severe withdrawal pains. The common response was conflict, apathy, and despair.

By 1955, with the construction of new factories in Bangalore for the manufacture of telephones, machine tools, aircraft, and radios, the village commenced a renewed assault upon the city. In 1952, one man from Namhalli was employed as a factory laborer. In 1960, there were 30 factory laborers and in 1966 there were over 100, with more than 30 employed in the telephone factory alone. As these laborers moved to company housing in the vicinity of their factories, the population of the village declined, and the growing labor shortage caused more and more landowners to plant their fields to casuarina trees, which could be sold for firewood. Namhalli obtained its first high school graduate in 1951; by 1966, every male child in the village was being groomed for a high school education. Many of the factories in Bombay and other cities require relatively little skilled labor, but the factories in Bangalore are almost entirely dependent on skilled labor. The jobs obtained by men from the village were therefore "long trouser" jobs paying a high salary and requiring a knowledge of English and other languages.

The wages brought home by workers commuting to the factory on company-owned buses were spent for urban clothing, bicycles, trips to the cinema, and improved housing. Much of the surplus cash was invested in "chit funds," money collected from a number of individuals and loaned at a monthly auction to whatever person will pay the highest rate of interest to use it for one month. The availability of comparatively large sums of money made it possible for Namhalli's farmers to develop irrigation wells and make other substantial investments in agriculture. A one-acre grape garden might require an investment of 10,000 rupees for a well and 5,000 rupees for grape plants and trellises, but in a few years the annual income from such a garden might reach five or ten thousand rupees. Five acres of millet land, on the other hand, might produce an annual profit of no more than 100 rupees plus food for the family.

In 1966, then, Namhalli was the beneficiary of a highly success-ful and evidently permanent entry into the urban environment. Economic and to a large degree political domination of the village had fallen into the hands of the telephone-factory workers. This power stemmed in part from their role as moneylenders and finan-ciers, but it also arose from their access through the company union to lawyers, doctors, and even cabinet ministers. Even the police now spoke respectfully to the telephone workers and considered them equals. Power and influence also resulted from the participa-tion of village members in a variety of government offices and urban institutions. The village bus conductor, government clerk, and taxi driver were in a position to exert some economic and political influence in the urban environment. Working through networks of friends, relatives, and fellow workers, individuals had easy access to hospitals, government bureaus, and the marketplace.

In the new situation, where one member of a family might be living outside the village, another working in a factory, and a third practicing agriculture, the tendency toward reduction in family size was reversed. Even where brothers divided their family estates, the brother who remained in agriculture tended to retain control of the family lands while the others stood by to provide cash and other assistance in emergencies. Where the joint family survived, its head ceased to be an absolute authority assigning different tasks to each of the male members and became an equal, cooperating with his brothers or sons simply because it was convenient to do so. Remaining members of an economically undivided family, the factory laborer had access to a free supply of food and the farmer had access to land not being farmed by the factory hand.

Increases in family size also resulted from bringing sons-in-law and brothers-in-law into the village. These newcomers, often poor men from less urbanized villages, played an increasingly important role in carrying on agriculture while the owners of village lands worked in factories. In American cities, where jobs may be obtained impersonally through a demonstration of skill or the presentation of a high school diploma, possession of a wide network of friends and relatives may be comparatively unimportant. In Bangalore, where some kind of personal contact is required in order to accomplish even so small a task as the purchase of a reliable wristwatch, networks of personal influence are of extreme importance. People who leave the village make a point of maintaining family and personal ties, and their marriages are contracted with a view toward establishing productive relationships with other families. Marriages to spouses from the less urbanized villages to the east insure a source of labor and cheap agricultural products; marriages in the city to the west provide access to urban markets, factories, and government offices. Although Namhalli's traditional pattern of marriage to cross-cousins and sisters' daughters has been altered in the direction of intensifying urban contacts, carefully arranged marriages to close relatives remain the established pattern. The incidence of marriage to close relatives in Namhalli is still between 30 and 40 percent of all marriages, almost as high as in Elephant.

Over the last few decades, Elephant, Gopalpur and Namhalli have thus made sometimes tenuous but in every case profitable adaptations to the new urban environment. While the adaptations made by Elephant and Gopalpur seem impermanent, the history of Namhalli suggests that once a village has entered the urban market, it will eventually find a stable relationship to it.

From another perspective, the survival of all three villages depends greatly on whether Indian modernization follows a pattern of intensive agriculture (as in Japan) or of extensive agriculture (as in North America). In Japan, as in Namhalli, modernization has so far led to the intensive cultivation of relatively small plots of land, which requires a heavy investment of labor and capital and makes possible the support of a relatively large rural population. In the United States, particularly in the grain-farming regions of the Middle West, government policies have encouraged the development of an extensive form of agriculture that is highly industrialized but requires relatively little labor. This kind of agriculture, based on the use of heavy machinery to cultivate and harvest large acreages with little manpower, may become established in the Gopalpur region. If that happens, it will cause massive migrations to the urban centers by those who are driven off the land. Since India's modern factories require relatively little labor, such a migration could lead to the development of urban poverty and unemployment to a degree unprecedented in other nations.

In 1966, when I was last in Elephant, Gopalpur, and Namhalli, India was in the grip of a serious drought. All three villages maintained some agricultural production, but serious famine and starvation were prevented largely as a result of their profitable relationships to the city. All had sufficient resources to purchase grain imported from the United States. Namhalli, which needed the least help, was the beneficiary of a school lunch program supported by the United States.

In the years following 1966, the government of India engaged in the widespread introduction of new high-yielding varieties of wheat, rice, maize, and sorghum. Within a little more than a year, these new varieties were planted on over 16 million acres of land. By the early 1970s, according to newspaper reports, India appeared to have achieved a food surplus. This rapid increase in food production, called the "Green Revolution," combined with the rapid adoption of various forms of birth control and family planning, has markedly altered the traditional relationships between South Indian villages and their environments.

The most immediate effect of the Green Revolution is the postponement of the time when increasing population may lead to a renewal of the disastrous famines that afflicted South India until the turn of the century. Although a few writers concerned with Indian problems have come close to suggesting that famine is a necessary means of reducing India's population to manageable size, more humane and less damaging forms of population control are obviously desirable. Presumably, the Green Revolution is a means of buying time in which to introduce such methods. In 1973, drought and widespread crop failure substantially reduced India's agricultural production. I cannot say whether this reflected an exhaustion of the benefits of the Green Revolution or was simply a temporary lapse.

The Green Revolution produces real dangers and serious ecological effects that could in the long run make the situation even worse than before. The new crops involve a heavy use of chemical fertilizers and insecticides, which could produce irreversible and damaging alterations in farmlands and in the biological processes that take place on them. Because the new crops lack genetic variability, the planting of large acreages to single strains of grain might lead to a situation in which a single widespread disease could destroy a crop completely.

In terms of urban ecology, rapid increases in production could lead to a disastrous collapse of grain prices. Large numbers of farmers might be unable to dispose of their grain in urban markets and forced to fall back on subsistence agriculture. Small farmers in particular would then be unable to purchase the chemical fertilizers and insecticides on which they had become dependent. In these and other ways, the Green Revolution, like so many other agricultural revolutions, would be especially favorable to farmers who control large acreages of land. This opens the possibility that wealthy farmers, such as the patrons of the Gopalpur region, might use their political and economic influence to drive poorer farmers off the land. The urban migration likely to be triggered by the Green Revolution may be so vast that by 1975 the displaced population would be large enough to man the entire industrial sector of the United States.

Various world crises introduce imponderables that make it difficult to predict the future effects of modernization on the South Indian village. In their organizational capacity and knowledge of the modern world, people in Namhalli appear to have adaptive advantages at least equal to those possessed by farmers and factory workers in more industrialized societies. Their success in penetrating the urban job market and in developing a labor-intensive and profitable form of garden agriculture has required substantial changes in traditional patterns of social and ecological relationships. Nevertheless, Namhalli remains a South Indian village. The image of the village deity, stolen during the troubles of the 1950s, has been replaced, and the old rituals are still carried on. Traditional concepts of dharma and karma still underlie daily life.

Namhalli's ability to modernize and at the same time remain distinctively South Indian may, of course, be simply an accident of circumstances, arising from a particular and limited set of ecological conditions. Still, it is tempting to conclude that Gopalpur and Elephant, and other South Indian villages as well, will find similar ways of adapting to the crises of modernity without losing their identity as villages or as representatives of a distinctively South Indian civilization.

Chapter 11

THE SEAMLESS WEB

In Elephant, an older companion of the Svamiji expresses his view
of the relatedness of things as follows:

The four things a man wants most are an umbrella when the sun is
hot, a baby from the womb, Basavanna to all, and mush when he is
hungry.

Basavanna came to the earth, first as a wild animal, then as a bullock,
and then as a man. His dung is required to make things grow, and he is
required for plowing. A house without cattle or buffalo is poor. Now we
have only a few cattle, and we are becoming poor. I may have a pair of
bullocks worth one thousand rupees, and they may die. If they do, we
must again bring bullocks. We can't live without his help. Like a child
beaten by its mother, we must come back crying "Mother."

Basavanna is like our mother.

There may be machines for plowing or butter made from seeds, but
machines are unreliable, and nothing is so good as clarified butter and
milk.

The four important things are cattle, buffalo, land, and rain. This part
of the world must depend on these things—we have no irrigation, no
industries, no business. We must believe in these four in order to live.

In South India, especially in Mysore, Basavanna reigns. In the
Gopalpur region, his stone image sits patiently outside the doorway
of every major temple. In Namhalli, they say, "All of the gods are in
the cow." Only a few miles away a great stone outcrop, the bullock-
shaped Nandi Hill, is worshiped as the guardian of the territory he

surveys. Where he reigns, Basavanna also toils as servant, pulling the farmer's plow and serving as surrogate mother to his children. The "four things a man wants most" are the same four things that lie at the center of the ecological web of South Indian civilization —solar energy, people, cattle, and grain.

Basavanna is the key element in the ecological system. The persistence of villages—of permanently settled communities—is made possible by the fact that South Indian farmers have been able to produce grain continuously on the same lands over a period of several thousand years without exhausting the fertility of the soil. It is the sacred dung of Basavanna that restores and maintains soil fertility. Because of a dense population, South Indian farmers have gradually eliminated the wild animals that provide a protein source for hunting peoples. Such domesticated animals as pigs, goats, and sheep yield part of the animal protein required for good nutrition, but for most people the major source of animal protein is the milk of the cow. Basavanna is "like our mother."

In gross terms, most people are farmers, most farmers raise grain, most people derive the bulk of their diet from grain and of their animal protein from milk. Thus, the South Indian ecological system is dominated by a symbiotic relationship among cereals, cattle, and human beings. Buf if "the four important things are cattle, buffalo, land, and rain," what is the point of the endless complexity of this civilization? What need is there for towns and cities, for the complex system of jatis, for a complicated world view, for extensive ritual activity, for all the other relationships and arrangements that make up the civilization?

A rough index of the scale of the farmer's contribution to the support of his civilization can be derived by considering the fate of his harvested grain. Traditionally, after harvest he heaps his grain on the threshing ground and measures out the amounts due to others: a scoop of grain in charity to all poor people present; several scoops to such Muslim, Jangama, Brahmin, and other priests as may be standing by; more scoops to the Blacksmith, Barber, Astrologer, Goldsmith, Washerman, and other specialists; and finally, a substantial portion in payment of taxes and interest. The remainder, perhaps one-third or one-half of the crop, is barely sufficient to support the farmer and his family through the coming year. Even so, much of it will be eaten by rats or insects, used to purchase clothing and other necessities, and expended for religious and recreational purposes.

Depending on the productivity of his fields, the farmer with his household actually consumes somewhere between one twentieth and one fortieth of the grain he produces. A considerably greater proportion, perhaps one tenth of the harvested crop, is consumed by other families in the village who render various services to him or depend on his charity. Another portion of the crop flows outward to neighboring villages in payment for products and services not available within his community. The bulk of his production is siphoned off, first to the town, then to the city, in the form of interest, taxes, religious obligations, and payments for goods and services.

Because each village is uniquely adapted to its particular natural and social environments, gross estimates of the flow of grain from village to city have little relevance to specific villages. An isolated and relatively unproductive village like Elephant may retain as much as 40 to 50 percent of its harvested grain, while a highly productive rice-growing village may retain only 10 to 20 percent. To some extent, this contrast can be explained by the unwritten rule that farmers must retain the minimum amount of grain required for their subsistence and continued productivity, but variations in the retention of grain are also created by the relative effectiveness of tax collection in different regions and by differences in farmers' demands for goods and services in exchange for their exported grain.

In modern times, with the payment of taxes in cash rather than grain, continuing inflation has substantially reduced the amount of grain lost to the farmer through taxation. On the other hand, government control of grain prices, often achieved by dumping large amounts of foreign grain on the market, can be regarded as a form of indirect taxation. Various kinds of governmental assistance as well as increasing opportunities to purchase manufactured goods constitute growing tangible return on the farmer's contribution to the support of cities and governments. Even so, from the farmer's perspective, the services he receives always seem very much less than the services he provides.

South Indian farmers pay as little as possible for goods and services and in taxes and interest. They are strongly conscious of exploitation and grumble about it constantly. In Namhalli, despite the many services received from city and nation, farmers say, "The government should be set afire" or "The government's idea of helping is to drop a man who has collapsed on the head of a man who is standing." In the Gopalpur region, constant unrest leads to frequent assaults on members of the investor class. Throughout South India, especially in rice-growing regions with large numbers of investors, peasant rebellions are probably as common today as they have been in the past. The farmer dreams of a "return" to a self-sufficient village community. The popularity of political-religious reformers like Mahatma Gandhi can be attributed in part to their advocacy of a return to the good old dharmic days.

Despite the constant grumbling and the manifest antagonism to government and civilization, there is evidence that the farmer is in fact an ardent supporter of the system. Successful peasant rebellions do not result in marked changes in his relationship to the civilization. People in Gopalpur express dependence on and affection toward those they regard as "good" patrons. Part of the farmer's commitment to the system arises from the fact that he sees himself as better off than the landless laborers who help to weed and harvest his crop. The same dharmic ideas that give rise to the farmer's yearnings for village self-sufficiency and independence also cause him to glory in his religious obligation to feed the rest of the world. In the very fact of his oppression he sees both an expiation of the sins he committed in previous lives and an opportunity for rebirth as a wealthy patron or a raja.

The farmer's willingness to part with large portions of his harvested grain without an immediate tangible return is one of the great strengths of South Indian civilization and helps to explain its persistence. The South Indian world view provides a convincing rationale for continued participation in its civilization, and there is no indication that it has been weakened or even very much changed by the influences of Islam, Christianity, or modernity. Because the civilization hinges on dharma and on the acts of faith dharma inspires, its survival must be attributed in part to the strength and greatness of its ideas.

Nevertheless, ideas alone cannot guarantee survival. This is especially true of ideas that lead the farmer to sacrifice some 50 or 60 percent of his grain crop to the support of cities and towns and of elaborate political and religious hierarchies. The bulk of the energy he produces seems to be dedicated to organizations and institutions that consume but do not produce energy. But it is an iron law of adaptation that relatively inefficient, or energy-wasting organizations and institutions will be replaced by more efficient structures. In these terms, the farmer's strong feeling that he receives little return on his investment must be the result of maya, or illusion, for in reality South Indian civilization permits and encourages his productive capacity.

Most obviously and tangibly, the existence of political organizations larger than the village permits the construction of massive irrigation works. The urban centers of the major South Indian states and kingdoms have always been close to large acreages of irrigated land. The same has generally been true for the large towns that serve as regional marketplaces and administrative centers. Gopalpur and Namhalli both benefit from irrigation works constructed and maintained by the national government. The best customers for the millet raised in Elephant are farmers from a nearby rice-growing region who prefer to sell their expensive crop and consume the cheaper and more nutritious millet.

Major increases in efficiency are also obtained through the free exchange of material goods, manpower, and ideas within the larger society. The local and regional specializations in crop production permitted by the South Indian marketing system enable each village and region to produce the crops best suited to its particular environment. For example, villages in the Gopalpur region do not grow cotton or weave cloth, presumably because other crops are more productive and because the low humidity and high temperatures of the region make cotton thread too brittle. Traditionally, they obtained woven cloth from a cooler, wetter region to the east. Although under conditions of self-sufficiency, even minor interregional trade might occur, only the marketplaces and the developed patterns of trade characteristic of civilization make possible large-scale exchanges of commodities among villages and regions. Most villages produce most of the crops they require for internal consumption, but many specialize in the production of such crops as sugarcane, rice, tobacco, cotton, betel leaf, and sweet potatoes. Specialization, which is made possible by widespread marketing systems, probably doubles the productive capacity of the South Indian farmer, and in some cases it makes possible the occupation of lands that could not be farmed on the basis of self-sufficiency.

Exchange among villages and regions also decreases the extent to which the farmer must protect himself against local crop failure. For example, a millet-growing village can expect almost complete crop failure at least once every five years. Consequently, an isolated village would have to maintain a two- or three-year supply of food grains, some of which might be wasted if the anticipated crop failure did not take place. However, villages with good access to urban markets, such as Namhalli or Gopalpur, need store grain for only short periods. In most years, the grain they do not consume domestically is sold on the market for cash. In the event of crop failure, they use the cash to purchase grain from regions of crop surplus. Here again, the existence of a marketing system probably doubles the farmer's productivity.

The many different ways in which South Indian civilization encourages and permits exchanges of labor among villages and regions also helps to account for the civilization's efficiency. Intermarriage within jatis facilitates adjustments of household and village populations to meet economic requirements, and a whole series of devices described in earlier chapters make agricultural labor available at harvesttime and during periods of peak labor requirements. The ability of the farmer to obtain labor by calling upon part-time specialists, relatives from other villages, and members of low-ranking jatis is critical to the maintenance of a high level of agricultural production. Considering that a farmer requires from ten to twenty laborers to harvest an ordinary field of grain, the increased productivity resulting from an assured supply of labor must be on the order of ten- to twentyfold. Because villages like Elephant, Namhalli, and Gopalpur do not have sufficiently frequent harvests to support large numbers of agricultural laborers, their productivity would be much reduced if they could not import labor from other villages within their regions and even from other regions. It seeems probable that in many parts of South India extensive grain agriculture could not be carried on at all in the absence of interregional mechanisms for the exchange of labor.

The movement of farmers and farm laborers from village to village and from region to region is facilitated by patterns of charity and hospitality enjoined by the South Indian world view. In 1952, Namhalli and other villages near Bangalore contributed large amounts of grain to support refugees from drought-stricken regions to the east. In both traditional and modern times, agricultural slack seasons and years of crop failure have also been occasions for the construction of roads, irrigation works, temples, and fortifications. Such public works are in effect a means of returning to farmers and farm laborers the grain collected as taxes and interest and, at the same time, of redistributing it to those forced by necessity to migrate in search of employment. The availability of temporary sustenance outside the village makes possible the efficient utilization of marginal lands and the maintenance of a stable agricultural work force during periods when indiivdual villages cannot support their populations. Again, the existence of the civilization substantially increases productivity.

The circulation of goods and people requires rapid and effective communication over large areas. Such communication gives the farmer access to a wide range of crops and agricultural techniques. A civilization comprising millions of people who share the same world view and speak the same or closely related languages also makes possible the accumulation and sharing of a wide variety of adaptive techniques. In every sphere of life, from housebuilding to medicine, the civilization multiplies the options available to the local community in solving the problems that confront it. The variety of crops traditionally grown in South Indian villages is several times greater than is characteristic of isolated and self-sufficient communities elsewhere in the world.

In most human societies a large part of the energy obtained through carrying out subsistence activities is expended in various forms of conflict. In South India too, vast energies have been expended in domestic quarrels, disputes among village factions, and, in traditional times, warfare between contending states. Within the civilization, the energy expended in this way has been reduced by eliminating some kinds of conflict, especially deadly encounters between neighboring villages, and by controlling and regulating other kinds. The presence of a religious hierarchy independent of state and national political structures has traditionally encouraged rules of warfare that mitigate the duration and severity of wars between states. Traditional wars tended to be relatively nondestructive ritualized conflicts between specialists and usually did not involve the people in rural villages.

The idea of dharma, in the sense of right action, and the prospect of imminent supernatural punishment for individuals and villages that failed to behave in accordance with dharma, have been effective means for resolving conflicts of all sorts. The faith that religious and political leaders possessed a superior knowledge of dharma has made it possible to resolve conflicts by appeal to progressively higher authorities. Conflicts of all sorts are always mitigated by the fact that all participants must eventually present an appearance of righteousness before a higher court of judgment.

One of the most striking features of South Indian public behavior is the willingness of all individuals, particularly individuals of high status, to assume the role of peacemaker and authority on dharma. The individual who feels himself wronged by his spouse, by a neighbor, or even by a cabdriver need only appeal to the crowd of bystanders, who then constitute themselves an informal court and hand down a verdict. The need to eliminate conflict and ill will before ritual activities can be carried out provides yet another means of mitigating conflict.

One of the characteristics of South Indian civilization and of all other agricultural civilizations is that the primary producer, the farmer, appears to contribute much more to the support of the civilization than he receives in return. The foregoing consideration of the more general impact of South Indian civilization upon the farmer suggests that in the case of South India the increases in productivity that can be attributed to the civilization far outweigh the costs of supporting it.

Although most South Indian kings have been dethroned and the civilization as a whole is subject to modernizing influences ranging from industrialization to unrestricted population growth, the basic relationships that have characterized the civilization for some two thousand years remain intact. Family and kinship structures are still strong; most marriages still take place between close relatives in the same jati; great rituals are still held; and Basavanna still rules the land. South Indian civilization bends but does not break before the winds of change. Its strength and resiliency stem from a world view that sees nature and humanity as a single entity in which all aspects of nature and all kinds of humanity unite to play their proper dharmic roles. When the farmer contributes his grain to a distant and largely invisible government, he does so in part because it is his karma, his fate and duty, to do so. When governments build irrigation works or open their granaries to starving villagers, they do so in part because it is their karma to do so. South Indian civilization survives because it represents a web of ecological relationships that greatly increase the efficiency and productivity of the farmers who support it. The strands of the web are held together by the principles of the South Indian world view—by the image of harmony, unity, and right action that is dharma.

Suggested Further Reading

Although the literature concerning South Indian civilization is extensive, there are few published works that deal directly with South Indian ecology. Systematic and detailed ecological research has recently been completed by Conrad Arensberg and Joan Menscher, and by Morgan D. Maclachlan. Hopefully, their work will be published soon.

Beals, Alan R. "Interplay Among Factors of Change in a Mysore Village," *Village India*, McKim Marriott, ed., pp. 78–101. Chicago: University of Chicago Press, 1955. A discussion of change and adaptation in Namhalli between 1877 and 1953.

Gopalpur, A South Indian Village. New York: Holt, Rinehart and Winston, 1962. A general description of Gopalpur.

"Conflict and Interlocal Festivals in a South Indian Region," *Religion in South Asia*, Edward B. Harper, ed., pp. 99–114. Seattle: University of Washington Press, 1964. Describes festivals in the Gopalpur region.

"Namahalli, 1953–1966: Urban Influence and Change in Southern Mysore," *Change and Continuity in India's Villages*, K. Ishwaran, ed., pp. 57–72. New York: Columbia University Press, 1970.

Beals, Alan R. and Morgan D. Maclachlan. "The Internal and External Relationships of a Mysore Chiefdom," *Journal of Asian and African Studies* 1: 87–99. Describes political relationships in the Elephant region.

Beals, Alan R. and Bernard J. Siegel. *Divisiveness and Social Conflict.* Stanford, California: Stanford University Press. Several chapters are devoted to a description of Namhalli.

Béteille, André. *Caste, Class, and Power*. Berkeley: University of California Press, 1965. Discusses the economic and social organization of a village in Tanjore, Madras.

Dube, S. C. *Indian Village*. Ithaca, New York: Cornell University Press, 1955. A description of an urban influenced village near the city of Hyderabad.

Epstein, T. Scarlett. *Economic Development and Social Change in South India*. New York: The Humanities Press, 1962. A thorough and classic study of two villages in Mysore State.

Frykenberg, Robert Eric. *Guntur District, 1788–1848; a History of Local Influence and Central Authority in South India*. Oxford: Clarendon Press, 1965. A detailed study of a Telugu speaking district.

Hiebert, Paul G. *Konduru: Structure and Integration in a South Indian Village*. Minneapolis: University of Minnesota Press, 1971. Not too much on environmental relationships, but a good study of a somewhat isolated village not far from Gopalpur.

Ishwaran, K. *Tradition and Economy in Village India*. London: Routledge and Kegan Paul, 1966.

Shivapur. London: Routledge and Kegan Paul, 1968. These two books provide a description of a large village in Northwestern Mysore.

Srinivas, M. N. *Religion and Society Among the Coorgs in South India*. Oxford: Oxford University Press, 1952. A study of the unique social institutions of a relatively isolated region in Mysore State. The author has also published numerous articles concerning a village near Mysore City.

Ross, Aileen D. *The Hindu Family in its Urban Setting*. Toronto: University of Toronto Press, 1961. A study of Bangalore.

Index

CPSIA information can be obtained at www.ICGtesting.com
Printed in the USA
BVOW11s1533031214

377489BV00006B/15/P

9 781412 842730